THE SKY IS BLUE

THE SKY'S BLUE

THE SKY IS BLUE

CHRISTINE HEUERMANN

CONTENTS

Acknowledgements

Thank you, my heavenly Father, for such an assignment. Thank you for always making the sky blue and for removing the veil so that I could see the blue sky no matter the season. I love you. I am grateful that you would use me in such a powerful way.

It is humbling.

Thank you to my dear sweet husband Dale. You have held me, believed in me, supported me, held me accountable along the way, told on me (to Steve), laughed with me and cried with me as I struggled through this process.

I am so glad that you are my husband.

Thank you to my friend and development editor, Steven Lowe. You helped me pry the top off my Pandora's Box, tame the contents, examine the contents and realize that I've had dominion over my story all along. You helped me shape what I wanted to share, you pushed me when I needed to share more deeply, and you helped me realize my dream of being an author. I am grateful for the day that God whispered into my ear that you would become my friend and partner. Thank you for all your hard work and your brilliance. I've come to appreciate your abilities as the God given gifts. I have been blessed by being the beneficiary of those giftings.

Many thanks to you my friend.

Christine Heuermann
www.BlessingMom.com

Thank you!

Thank you to those that made a gift to me to help finish this
project:
Eric Heuermann
Brad Smith
Dan & Leslie Klassen

Preface

I remember when I first thought of writing this book. Years had already passed since my grand escape from the marriage sentence I was in. Still, what an unnerving and scary prospect it seemed. I felt physically nauseous for a moment. But I can be a bit stubborn. I think that sick feeling actually motivated me to do it even more. It started with a tug on my heart from God; a "tug" that grew into a clear call to use my voice and experiences of abuse to help anyone that might be existing in the same kind of life. But there were serious concerns. The largest of those being as a mom to 3 wonderful daughters I, of course, didn't want to see them get tangled up in any possible negative impact. That wouldn't be fair to them. I had some sleepless nights... a lot of them. It was, like most life challenging choices, a risk that required much prayer, consideration and support.

I started going through my journals - pages of life, thoughts, and emotions screaming memories of my past back at me. As unsettling as it was, it also served as a reminder of the good life I now live and an old friend, my therapist, who made a deal with me to put my thoughts on paper. I owe him a lot. As expected, it was arduous deliberately rummaging through my past, sifting through the pain of a very specific, yet common, type of abuse.

I don't have a PhD or other comparable credentials that might make me more qualified to tell this story. I simply lived it. Just like 10's of thousands of so many others. So, I wrote it... this book. I was fortunate to have some very special people, God brought across my path, who helped. They kept me motivated and feeling loved throughout the process. This account of my experience had to be told and told again by anyone and everyone that has ever encountered abuse. Until no one is left suffering alone.

As you get ready to take this journey with me, rather you're a survivor of an abusive relationship, in an abusive period of life, or a concerned loved one - I believe and hope you'll walk away forever changed. The moments I share are personal, and honest, delving into some of the most private days of my life, innermost thoughts, and an abusive marriage of 20 years. A life of circumstances brought on by choices I made as well as choices made by others. This is not a declaration of victimization but a coming out of the shadows of false shame, and a much needed change in personal and social perspective. Control and manipulation are stealth forms of abuse in many relationships, hard to recognize, and easy to rationalize until it has consumed you.

I couldn't see beyond the survival of the moment. Individuals caught in abuse know the secret self-whispers of, "*I can survive this next moment.*" Depression is a prevalent factor - playing a debilitating role. When I finally looked up, years had passed. In it all I could never imagine a life beyond the condition I was living in and I certainly couldn't imagine sharing my story with anyone. Who would listen? I spent years embarrassed and ashamed of the life I was living and "allowing". Questioning myself, while pieces of me disappeared. I was hiding in plain sight - covering it up like a blemish on my skin. That had to change. I had to seek change. God had a better plan for my life.

Now, I can't imagine not sharing my story. Through sharing bits and pieces over the years, it has helped so many people. It's helped me, as well. It's removed the stigma I, and others, had about what abused individuals look like. We aren't weak. As a matter of fact, I believe we're some of the strongest people you know. It's my hope that this book will help those currently in an abusive relationship to find a way out, and those seeing the signs will never have to live through it at all.

It is often when circumstances seem the most hopeless that you are ripe for God's miraculous deliverance. We have a part to play. That part can sometimes just be saying to yourself, "No. You don't get to do that to me anymore." It may be hard for you to believe, but change is accessible and possible. Looking back over all the time spent putting my life back together, I feel nothing but joy and peace. As you'll see in this book, chapter to chapter, I refer to my abuser by using different names and titles. I associated him to these references as I saw him through the years and how I see him now. That takes perspective, something we don't necessarily have while in a traumatic situation. We must give ourselves the life we were meant to live. You're undoubtedly worth it. We need to give ourselves the space and time to work through things and heal. It's absolutely worth it.

CHAPTER 1

I Have a Friend Who

It comes out of nowhere... or maybe you were on a collision course with it for years. Life happens and it dances a hard jig on our sensibilities and logic. It happens to you. It makes you think thoughts - lots of thoughts. And they aren't all good... or real. But you deal until you come up for air with whatever little fight you have left in you... because life is worth it. There has to be more! You escape. I escaped. And I think I have a story to tell but who would want to hear it? Maybe I deserved it, maybe I was just weak, and maybe it wasn't as bad as I thought - but you know deep in the psychological and emotional scaring that it was. You know it was. But what if, what if? Can I do this? Will I do this? It's going to be embarrassing to put yourself out there, scary to let everyone in, and risky, even unsafe. What will people say? There are lots of unknowns attached to full disclosure and truth. And you know this - I did too. All great reasons to duck for cover. Or stand your ground and pray for the best. Or both? I considered all of the above even as I write.

Anyway... "I want to tell you about a woman I know - a friend. Her name is Rebecca. I don't know what happened but Mr. Wonderful a.k.a her husband really went off the deep end this time. She must have upset him, done something seriously wrong because he---". That's how I would start my stories. It was harmless - I wanted to fit in. I wanted to feel relief. I wanted to live. I wanted someone to tell me I wasn't crazy... I mean, tell Rebecca. It could be anything; something Rebecca needed to talk about or work out so that at the very least she didn't lose her mind. Oh, the stories I could tell you about the horrible marriage she had. The betrayal she suffered or the horribly degrading, embarrassing things that happened to her. She was so stupid, always making her husband angry... rarely knowing how.

> I was slowly losing myself and I had no one to tell. And he knew it. That was the plan after all.

Consequently, I created Rebecca my closest and dearest friend. What a horrible life she was living, with seemingly no way out. She lived an existence of self-loathing, internal conflict, rejection, loneliness, confusion, hardship, deception, abuse, more abuse, emotional bondage, and cruelly inflicted indignities. Now to be clear, Rebecca is not perfect but you do what you have to, to survive. No excuses. She was a mess. I suppose we're all a little messy at times. She was, however, the perfect "out". I use to feel --- I mean my friend felt, I mean... it got confusing. There's a personal price we pay to hide behind a "Rebecca" for too long. I grew tired of being made to feel insignificant and invisible... but that was the least of my concerns.

Which brings me to this point, have you ever started a

story with "I have a friend who…" or maybe asked a question that began with that same "friend" needing some advice? Okay, sometimes there really is a friend in need but often, for me anyway (maybe for you too), there wasn't. We all have our reasons for why we use our "friend". I found an element of freedom in using mine. I did it often - got good at it. The suggestive laughter and sarcastic inference of "Right, a friend" were warranted by those I felt comfortable enough to let into my friend's life (yeah, think about that statement for a second), but I'd laugh it off just the same. It's what we do. The charade has to look real or what's the point? Well, if that scenario seems way too familiar in your own life, then you'll understand why my story has to begin there.

I have a friend who… I use to hide behind at one time in my past. She was my voice when I was afraid to speak or needed courage to vent. When I feared judgment, from those who should have had no power over me, she came to my rescue. She was to blame when I couldn't stand to look at myself… when I felt like I should do something but was (in my mind at the time) too weak or afraid to try. I bring "her" up because, even now, I struggle with the idea of using my friend while writing to you. Old habits die hard. Don't they? But I can't. I've spent too many years doing that already. This is my voice; this happened to me - not Rebecca - same as it's happening to so many of you. My life, your life, deserves better than to be cloaked under a nonexistent third-party. The expression of my truth, this truth, is a lifeline for all who wish to grab hold of it. But hold on tight because as we all know, though truth is not supposed to fear challenge - it doesn't mean it's easy.

Unfortunately and tragically, mine is not an uncommon story. That said, my story (maybe like yours) is not, as I've said, one that's easy to tell. But this is true of most challenges in life that require calling out the "wrongs" people do, and hoping to bring change to those still living as sufferers of that wrong. I once lived under a mindset of false shame, too frightened to say the things I have to say in the pages to come. If you care at all about what others think (and even the most frozen heart has someone they wish cared) there's a lot of pressure, thought, concern - whatever you want to call it, as to what you reveal, and what "they" (friends, family) know. More importantly, what will they do with what they know? Will they hold it against me, judge me, think I'm crazy, and look at me differently through a well-meaning smile? I'm not sure. I wasn't sure. So, I kept it to myself for many years. Better to suffer alone than risk the stares of my friends and family. Honestly, looking back now, I don't think they cared much to know anyway. It made things easier on all of us. Just thinking about saying something my pulse would elevate, my breathing would change, and I'd get a little sweaty. I was so fearful to tell them - to say the word, "Help". Because then what? What came next? I decided to play it safe. Let Rebecca take the hit! Let the opinions fly, without holding back, (without much thought I might add, and sometimes with alcohol involved - let's be truthful). Besides, I was gossiping about me. No one was getting hurt; Rebecca lived far, far away where no one could get to her. Once the topic was put out there, on poor Rebecca's behalf, and everyone had weighed in, it didn't always go the way I had hoped but exactly how I had feared. I began to realize that I made the right call to keep it under the heading of "A friend who..." Confusing, yes, but in some ways a very freeing decision. Look, I just didn't want to lose my mind. I was happy that it was she and not I living that tragic, pathetic life, even if just for that moment. I was free.

I think the part I have the hardest time reconciling is why? Not the basic reasoning - I'm clear on that - the repercussions, etc. I'm trying to settle why we have to jump through the hoops at all if we truly care about one another? I believe it's safe to say most automatically accept and assume that there's probably no "friend", when we stop to think about it. But we're all so damn polite. No one ever wants to pry. In defense of those who truly care, maybe their lives are just so crazy and complicated too that who needs an extra burden to shoulder, to pray about. Right? Or is that still wrong? Anyway, the people we hang out with are supposed to be our friends, our family. I assume they mean well. I know I mean well when I weigh in on these types of conversations. No judgment - I've done it countless times. I'm just amazed at the posturing that I've done with others (and to others) to protect myself instead of just being who I really am and seeing things for what they really are. Seems we're all trying to figure it out as we go. One thing that is for sure, we're all in that boat together.

I knew what writing this meant; a journey back to places that I had left, put away, having to revisit painful memories that I wanted to forget not reexamine. But some things are worth doing for the good that will follow. I couldn't bring myself to hide behind "A friend who..." anymore. I didn't want to lie to you. If I'm to claim a quick victory here (besides my found optimism - it's a God thing), I've learned to really listen. The answer may be inconvenient at times but if you speak to me about a "friend" - I'll be paying attention. I know the rules to that game well.

Thank you Rebecca for being my persona but I'll take it from here.

CHAPTER 2

When We Met

(PRINCE CHARMING)

It's summer! I'm sixteen and just started my new job at a restaurant-slash-diner... there's actually a funny story attached to how I got it. My friends and I made up a jingle, and sang it to the General Manager, a couple months ago. When I came back, and applied for the server position, I reminded him - he hired me on the spot. Yeah, for me, it's a super cool place to work. The polyester brown uniforms kind of make me feel important. We have a salad bar with a sneeze guard; I get to help keep everything looking nice. There's a greasy haze that just kind of hangs in the air from the grill, where the steaks are cooked, smells good... I like steak. I love my job because all the people who work here are friendly with each other and all of us work hard. Like a family, I guess. It gives me money and a sense of freedom; two things that make me feel like a grownup.

There's this guy who came into the restaurant today. Let's call him... Prince Charming. I don't know his name yet, but I will. He's nice looking and all the girls seem to think so too. He certainly thinks so. But that's okay. He tries to act like he doesn't, but he does; I can tell by the way he looks up from under his eyelashes. It reminds me of something a girl might do to a guy. It's like he's looking to see who's looking. Well, I'm looking, and he sees me doing it too. I blushed, looked away and hurried to get back to work. This is good. I feel excited inside, but I don't want to get my hopes up... but I do... because it's fun.

Prince Charming comes mostly every day to eat. He's dressed in his military fatigues; I don't know what branch he's in. He's tall, slender, short dark-black hair, clean cut with a groomed moustache and he has a southern drawl. Oh, that southern drawl...he can get whatever he wants just by talking. His voice is slow and steady, almost hypnotic and it wraps around my mind and... I turn to mush. He's charming and pays attention to me (wait, why me?) by asking me to do little things for him, special favors, and then says, "Thank you", and flashes that flirty smile at me while I am working. He tips me - at a restaurant that people don't normally tip. I think he might like me. He really doesn't say a whole lot other than small talk. Mainly "Hello" or "Can you get me--"this or that. It's the "Please" and "Thank you" he says directly to me, like he means it, that gets to me. I'm not used to the attention, but I am soaking it up and thrilled with every moment. I want to make sure that he doesn't ask anyone else so; I rush to do what he wants. I want to make sure no one else gets in on what I have going with him. He looks directly into my eyes and smiles. My heart beats just a little bit faster in a good kind of way. I feel like I'm living in a romance novel...

I found out today that Prince Charming is for sure from the south and displaying all the charms of a southern gentleman. He introduced himself to me and all I can say is "Wow!" He shook my hand and held on a little bit longer than normal, before letting go. He meets all my requirements: He has a real "regular" job, check! A car, check! Seems to be reliable, check! Doesn't do drugs, check! And, as I believe I've covered sufficiently, he's good looking too, double check!! He's so nice to me... I am so lucky! I really think he likes me a lot because he just asked me out!

The girls at work are all jealous and that's okay. I've never really had that happen before. One of the girls said something to me about him being too old for me. I told her she was just jealous because he wasn't interested in her. There's another girl at work he seemed slightly interested in. He asked me about her when her family came in for dinner. He said, "So who are all those people cutting up and carrying on with her?" I said, "They're her family. They come in like once every couple of weeks and embarrass the crap out of her, but I think she likes it. Must be nice to have a family like that." He asked me, "What you don't have any family?" I said, "Yeah I do but they are pretty much crap. We don't really get along and I don't live with them or have much to do with them. Gotta go... the boss is eyeballing me." His interest was turned from her and really increased in me. It seemed kind of strange, but whatever her loss and my gain.

I realize it was at this point, he saw the perfect host in a detached, naïve sixteen-year-old girl.

Looking back now, I gave him all the information he needed. I was perfect for his brand of person. I wish I had someone to tell me, "Look before you leap" - my heart had leaped, and my life was changed forever. We started seeing each other outside of my work. I didn't have the constraints of high school, it being summer. All my spare time was spent with him. The subject of school never came up. His work schedule was full time, so I just made myself available when he wasn't working. I was pretty much up for anything, which involved a lot of exploring the area because he wasn't from there. He was living in an efficiency motel with a drive in behind it, so we would watch movies for free by just tuning in the radio to listen. It was cool, kinda, "our thing" and private. When it came to doing group things he never wanted to participate, and I was never really sure why. Prince Charming always makes everything sound okay. It doesn't really take much convincing on his part though; I want my Prince to love me, so whatever he wanted he could have.

We had sex for the first time. I'll spare you the embarrassing details, all except this one moment. He was really weird about making sure he had a "raincoat". He left me midway through, put his clothes back on, and left in search of a, "raincoat". I'm lying there thinking, "What does he need a raincoat for? It's not raining." When he came back, he explained he couldn't find any... now I am super confused. I asked him, "What do you need a raincoat for? It's sunny outside." He laughed at me. I immediately felt stupid and self-conscious but still didn't know what he meant. He said, "Condom. A raincoat is a condom. I can't believe you've never heard it called that." I said, "Oh, well I haven't. You know, I'm on birth control." "Really? Do you have the pills on you?" he asked. "No, they're at home. Why?" He said, "Well, I'm not doing it if you can't prove you're on them." Turns out that stand was short lived, and we did it... we had sex.

I was sitting on Prince Charming's lap one lazy day, kissing, and talking in between. He asked me, "So, when are you going to get a full-time job and quit playing around?" I laughed and said, "I've got to finish high school first." He stood up and I went to the floor with a thud. It was like something you see in a comedy except he wasn't laughing... and then neither was I. He was freaked out that I was underage. How could Prince Charming not know? He said accusingly, "You know I can go to jail for being involved with you! The military can charge me with fraternizing [with a minor] and I can get kicked out or worse! You've been lying to me!" He was not happy. I asked him, "Well, how old are you? And I haven't lied to you, you never asked!" He was nearly seven years older than me. I was a little surprised how much older he was. I scrambled to make sense of it. I said, "Um, didn't I tell you that no one cares? Who am I going to tell? Who exactly is going to tell on you? It certainly won't be me. I mean, seriously we never go out with anyone else. So, other than a few people that I may have said something to who the hell knows?" Those were the right words. Good, he calmed down. That's what was important. He believed me and everything was okay again. I didn't understand what had happened. I hadn't experienced that side of him before. He was fine one second and lost it the next. Then back to normal... business as usual. In my immature mind I was thinking, "It's the eighties for Pete's sake no one cares about this stuff anymore...do they?"

I have to take a personal moment here, please indulge me. Part of me wanted to believe Prince Charming didn't know I was underage, but I was never fully convinced. I've asked the question many times over the years, wouldn't a typical person end it after finding that out? The obvious answer is, "Yes". But, as I now argue that point with myself, it almost seems trivial. Not in the sense that it's unimportant. It is without debate morally and lawfully troubling. I mean, "trivial" in comparison to the bigger picture - who he was; his perception of others, me. His mindset and rationale made his intent clear. So, to argue the point of age discrepancy now would be the logical equivalent to burying the "lead" as they say. It was part of the plan.

If I could go back and have a conversation with my sixteen-year-old self today, I'm not exactly sure I'd listen to me, but I'd try... hard. I'd say, "I know dating a grown man makes you feel, grown up, and even special. You need to feel that... I know all too well. You're having unprotected sex with him, have you thought about the consequences of that decision? Has he? It's going to cost you in ways you don't understand yet. He obviously doesn't care about the consequences. You should be asking, "Why?" Why doesn't that matter to him? Because those that never take responsibility for their actions, don't have to worry about the outcome; they just blame others or lie their way out if it. What do you really know about him? You know so little yet you're willing to give yourself over to him. An ounce of validation is all you think you're worth? You don't have to rush into "love". You are not what the voices inside of you say you are. Trust me - you're beautiful and strong and funny and so special. It'll happen one day with the right man... who'll respect you. If only you could believe in yourself long enough to see the future. Please hold on.

Could you just consider, for a moment, there might be something wrong with him; he finds a sixteen-year-old girl to be a "win"? Okay, so, he never wants to be around any of your friends... so what? That's not at least a light-red flag? There are laws to protect minors and that's what you are, like it or not. Your Prince Charming has just blown past any consideration of those laws, like they don't exist! He said "I loves you" - he didn't mess around. He brought out the heavy artillery, early on. The words any woman wants to hear, especially if they aren't sure they can or should be loved. Do you really even know what love looks like, yet? What do your friends have to say? Are you talking with them - listening to anyone? You have friends who really care about you, what are they saying? Do they even know about him? Don't isolate. Don't ignore the signs. Please hold on until you mature a little more. You are worth so much more than you know right now - 16 is hard, but it's about to get harder.

I thought that being an adult was much better than being a "kid". I did everything to portray myself as an adult. I had kissed my childhood goodbye and was full steam ahead towards adulthood. I wanted the freedom and the control of making my life my own. I was eager to fall in love with anyone who could paint the picture of love and acceptance I was looking for. I wanted the fairytale happy ending... Hell, in truth, I wanted the entire Fairy Godmother, wand waving, pixy dust flying, pumpkin changing, horse-drawn coach, and shimmering glass slipper, Cinderella story. And why not? Where is it written that young girls can't have that? I wanted to be happy. Life had already shown me enough of the stuff that makes you strong. My Prince Charming was doing a fine job with his paintbrush.

I'm seeing what I need and want to see. It may all be lies but...the land of delusion was so much more enticing.

We're having a great summer. We've been going to the lake and hang out with some of his friends. That's a positive change. We go shopping and out to eat too. I feel like we talk about everything under the sun and we have so much in common. I listen to every word he says. Every word. I say it that way because I am really trying to learn and understand everything about him. I think that's what people do when they want to love someone. We talk about what we want for the future and about knowing Jesus. I let him do most of the talking because I'm trying to get to know him and what he likes. We don't seem to differ on any subject because I don't want to differ on any subject with him. I want to want what he wants. I'm convincing myself that everything he wants is good and it's okay not to want anything for myself unless he wants it for me. I made things so easy for him. I think I'm keeping up.

I am falling in "love". I say "love" because it's a sixteen-year-old girl's version of love and because of my brokenness and messed up family life. I had a very skewed picture of love because of my family's divorce. I'm just happy to be with him. I don't ever remember feeling this way before. I am overwhelmed with his love. I want him to meet my family... isn't that what you do when you're in love with someone? I never hid my family from Prince Charming. I told him all the sordid details of my messy family dynamics. I, of course, shared this through a youth-colored lens but I did tell him. What I didn't realize was that I was doing reconnaissance for him. I had the chance to go visit my mother and my brother who lived a couple of hours away. I have invited Prince Charming to join me. He surprised me and accepted. We went and stayed for a few days at my mother's house.

While we were there an ex-boyfriend of mine decided he wanted to win back my affections and sent me not one but two-dozen long stem roses. They were absolutely beautiful. Prince Charming, with ice in his voice said, "Throw them away now." I stood my ground. I replied, "I won't. These flowers won't win me back, but I will not waste something so beautiful. I will, however, throw the card away." I put the roses on top of the refrigerator, in the kitchen, hoping the heat would shorten their life. It was the only concession I was willing to make. Oh, and I put bleach in the water - not realizing that would extend their life. Those flowers stood there, mocking him for days. Secretly, I wanted him to know I was a catch. Someone else thought I was worth enough to try to "win me back".

Overall the trip was fun, despite the "great rose incident" as I came to refer to it later on. On the car ride back, I was informed by Prince Charming that he was never going to buy me flowers or feel like he had to compete with anyone for my attention ever. I guess I should have just thrown the flowers away, but they sure were beautiful. My mom told me later that those roses lasted for almost a month. God sure does have a sense of humor when He's trying to get us to realize something. I believe God was trying to tell me that I was worth more than what I was getting. The problem was I just wasn't listening to God.

It was getting towards the end of the summer when I met one of Prince Charming's sisters. I was immediately smitten with her. She looked like she walked out of a magazine or catalog. Her hair, makeup, jewelry... she was all put together. A woman of the world and she seemed nice to me. She complemented me. She gave me pointers on girl things. She told me she would be happy to take me under her wing and show me the way. I wonder what she meant by that. She too has that southern drawl that's intoxicating. Her voice has an edge to it, though it's not quite as smooth as Prince Charming's voice. I know it's silly to be so impressed but I am. I really like her. She could easily be the big sister I never had. I like that feeling.

Princess Charming is very generous, she gives me gifts and seems not to have a problem with my age whatsoever. She told me that I don't have to wear much make up yet but someday I will and when I do, she will show me how to put it on. She kind of wears a lot of it but she can pull it off. How did she learn all that stuff? I mean, it's got to be exhausting to do all that hair, make-up, clothes and jewelry and, and, and...whatever. I've had fun with her while she's been here and Prince Charming seems really, really close to her. Whatever she tells him, he listens to and does. And under her guidance...

My Prince Charming, asked me to marry him today. It was on the sidewalk outside his motel door. Well, he didn't really ask me. He handed me a box and said, "Open it." I opened it and looked at him. He raised his eyebrows. I of course said, "Yes!" I love him so much and can't imagine living without him. I feel like the good luck fairy has blessed me! He said,

"The ring will have to do, it's all I could afford." I said, "I love the ring, it's perfect." And just like that - my Prince Charming left, six weeks of summer went by so fast and now he was on his way back to the military base he's been assigned to. I'm so sad. I miss him already. I don't know how I'm going to make it through until I see him again. He's going to be so far away. He promised I'll see him again at Christmas but that's such a long time. He promised we'd talk on the phone and write. How romantic... I'll get love letters!

A lot has happened and is happening. It seems so fast but I'm ready to be grown up and have my own life, my own family. I moved back to my mom's house and started the process of preparing for marriage. I went back to high school too. School seemed so boring after the summer I had. The students seemed like such children. I'm not going to say I felt superior, I just felt very different and very far away from them like I couldn't relate anymore.

I didn't get love letters... but I did get cards. He sent humorous cards. I'm already learning to say, "Well, it's better than nothing" and laugh to myself. I'm trying not to be disappointed. It's stupid. I'm not normally needy. Is it wrong to want a romantic letter or just one card that expresses real feelings? He would send me junk mail because our names were on it together, and he'd remind me that I would be Mrs. Prince Charming soon. He was good - no, actually masterful at knowing just when and what to say to stop me from talking about what I was really feeling. Prince Charming baited me like that. I continually took the bait. He would call but we wouldn't talk for long, he'd always remind me that the phone bill would be too expensive. I knew that was true. I understood... but I didn't - if you know what I mean? My brain and my heart were battling. He would get on the phone just long enough to ask me "What are you planning on doing for work?" or something equally romantic, remind me that he was coming for Christmas, and then get off the phone. Christmas couldn't come soon enough.

I just got off the phone with Prince Charming. He told me he left the military. What? He never even told me he was considering leaving or that he didn't like the military. In all fairness, I never really asked, I assumed he liked it. Today was the first I had heard anything contrary to my assumption. I don't exactly know how to feel. It seems sudden, and out of nowhere. Should I be happy for him, supportive, concerned, sad? Oh crap, should I be worried (it was going to be our security)? Do I have the right to even ask why? After all, we're going to be Mr. and Mrs. Prince Charming - he said so. So, I asked, and he responded, "I don't like being told what to do and how to do it by people who are not as smart as me." "Oh. Well, I never heard you talk that way before about your job in the military. Was there something going on?" I asked him. "No more than any other day. The people above me get there by kissing somebody's ass and I am not going to kiss anybody's ass, you hear me?!" I said, "Yeah, I hear you but I'm not asking you to kiss anybody's butt I'm just asking why you left the military?" Can I ask that?

Okay, wait! There's that feeling again. I always feel like I'm intruding in someone else's relationship. Okay, back to it...

"I'm sick of all the bureaucratic bullshit and waste and no

one is going to tell me what to do. It was getting time to reen-
list so my superiors said I could combine any unused leave
time and get out early. So, I did. I am now at my parents'
house." I said, "Ok, so...what are you going to do now? Do
you have any ideas for work? Why didn't you tell me what was
going on?" He replied, "Ahh, I don't know what I am going
to do right now... I'm just going to relax and figure it out. I'll
let you know." And that was that. He hung up the phone like
he had something better to do. He never did answer my question as to why he never shared his discontent with me, or any
of his personal struggles for that matter. It made me feel like
it was none of my business. Maybe I shouldn't have asked. I'll
spend the next several hours making excuses for his behavior.
It'll be okay.

The months came and went and before long it was Christmas time. My Prince Charming came bearing gifts. Arms full
of presents! What a teenager's delight! I was so happy to see
him! It felt like forever since I had seen him! What a happy
Christmas! We celebrated and went out dancing and eating
and even a little drinking - even though I wasn't supposed to.
We sent out the old year and brought in the New Year talking
about the exciting things coming in the year ahead.

My mom noticed that I was sicker than normal and said
something to me about, "I better not be pregnant." I went,
bought, and took a pregnancy test and found out that I was. I
felt immediate panic. What was I going to do?

CHAPTER 3

Misconceived Conception: My Abortion

(HEARTACHE)

Misconceived: A verb - Failed to understand correctly. Judge or plan badly, typically on the basis of faulty understanding. Yeah, I know. I figured that part out.

I was hopelessly naïve. What I would give to go back in time and have a conversation with my 16-year-old self. My head was in the clouds... or somewhere else. Head in the clouds... or shomewhwre else. I thought I had it all figured out. I just knew everything was going to be alright. We're engaged, and in love and this baby represented our love. Maybe this wasn't planned or the perfect timing but in my mind it's manageable. So I practiced, even daydreamed about his acceptance of the news...

"Hey! Guess what? We're pregnant!"

"Well, you're not going to believe this but..."

"So, what if I told you, you were going to be a dad?"

"We better step-up the wedding because we're going to be a family."

"I have some amazing news…" Yup, that's the one!

Hopeful, I called him…

As it turns out, everything is not alright. He shouted that feeling right out of me. How wrong I was, thinking everything was going to be. I immediately found myself on the defensive. He accused me, "How could you have let this happen? Why weren't you using birth control? How could you be so irresponsible?" Minutes in I wasn't talking about the baby or family - I was protecting my reasoning for not being on birth control. "When I moved back home - I no longer had access…" I said. He knew this, right? I questioned myself. It's my fault - his use or lack of use of a "Raincoat" was not to be questioned. I can't believe he's acting this way. He's scolding me like a parent ashamed of his child's actions but was the one having sex with me… marring me.

Stunned by his anger, my heart breaking, I stumbled over my words. I immediately felt vulnerable, because he said he loved me, and stupid because I believed him. The tears streamed down my face. My shame and now embarrassment, he sees I'm a stupid child; I was relieved he couldn't see me crumpled on the stairs holding the phone. He's breaking down any walls of defense and self-respect I thought I had. Quietly crying, holding it in, I asked him, "What am I supposed to do?" I found myself making excuses for him, like; maybe he's just scared too. He'll come around to the idea of having a baby. He just needs to think about it.

My heart hurt… it was broken.

Heartache explained, "You've got it all wrong, it wouldn't be fair to bring a baby into a new marriage." I empathized, "I know you're probably scared; I am too. We're going to get married anyway, why does it matter?" He went on to say, "I won't do this to my family."

THERE IT IS! The truth. It's not about being fair to our child, or to us, our love - it was always about the family. I would soon realize how skilled Heartache was at keeping up "appearances".

"What do you mean to your family?" I said. "It would be too hard on them. It would mess up all my plans for the future. The best thing you can do is just get rid of it." He just said, "it". He said, "It's just easier this way." He was in full control of the conversation. Heartache assured me he would send the money to take care of it I just need to find out how much. He made it all sounded so logical. Overwhelmed by all my feelings and thoughts, I found myself agreeing with him. I didn't know what else to say or do to slow things down. I was not equipped to go back and forth with him. On and on he went until I was back to agreeing with him and his plans. I was afraid and alone - the one person I thought would be on my side was telling me he wasn't. I came to realize that he used the tactic of overwhelming me to control my responses. Manipulation is a psychological tool best used on the young and ill-prepared. I qualified.

I wasn't a victim... I was the poster child.

I hung up the phone and put my head against the receiver and cried again. There had to be another way. I felt like I had been run over. My heart heard that he didn't really care but that just couldn't be true because he said he loved me. I decided to cover over that spot in my heart for now and tried to forget about it.

It seems weird to me now that I could just schedule the abortion. I couldn't vote, get married, join the military, buy a gun or schedule a medical procedure without an adult's consent but this one thing I could. Anyway, I had to go for an ultrasound to make sure I was still in the window of opportunity to have an abortion. When it was explained to me that's why I was there, part of me was secretly praying that they would tell me I couldn't have one. I hadn't really thought that through though because it would've caused a whole bunch of other problems. While the technician was performing the ultrasound, I asked her questions about what I was seeing on the screen. She kept looking at me strangely. I can only guess but I imagine girls who are planning on having abortions don't ask a lot of questions about what's on the screen. I wanted to know because I was hoping I could use it to persuade Heartache to change his mind. I don't know for sure, but she probably wasn't supposed to tell me what I was looking at; where the heart was, if I could hear the heartbeat, stuff like that. I swear I could feel the heartbeat in my face, as it was turning red. I thought to myself, "I don't know if I can really do this. This is a little person. God, can you please save me from this? God, will you make him change his mind?" The technician delivered the bad news. I was still able to go through with the abortion.

I called Heartache to see if I could get my Prince Charming back... I wanted to save the baby. I'm wrestling with this decision that was decided for me. I tried sharing what I learned at the ultrasound. He didn't care. When that didn't work I went onto begging, crying, manipulation. Whenever I called Heartache, he'd up his game. He knew how to apply pressure. He would say, "We've talked about this. We're done if you don't do it. So, you decide. I love you." I didn't want to be done. I wanted it my way. I didn't understand why I couldn't have both. I could never get him to just talk about it. There was never any conversation. He always spoke in absolutes, but the absolutes always made me feel stupid or lucky he still wanted to include me in his life - that was supposed to be our life. Then he would top it off with "I lovvve youuu...." all drawn out and sweet. He would say, "We have a plan and you're trying to mess it up. What is wrong with you? You made a small mistake it's okay. I forgive you. I have a great life waiting for you. All you have to do is this one little thing. I've given you the means to do it so do it already" I really want a great life... why was this the cost? I don't feel like I have a great life right now. Everything seems like such a mess and I'm miserable.

Heartache didn't live in the same state. So, when it was time for me to go to the abortion clinic I went alone. I don't think it would have mattered if he lived in the same house. It would have taken great effort and character for him to be there with me. I really wanted him to be there. I needed him to be there and I told him so. I just needed Heartache to show, in some tangible way, that he really loved me - not just words. Heartache made his case that it would be ridiculous for him to take the time off to make a special trip for this. He explained, "It's just a simple medical procedure. Girls do it all the time."

He asked me, "Why are you making such a big damn deal about it? "He went on to say, "Quit being such a baby about it." What I wanted to say was, "I am making a big damn deal about it because I don't want to do it and you're not listening to me!" I never did... I couldn't.

There was no way I could ask my mom - we weren't close, and I felt like she just wanted it to be like it never happened. It just made me feel more ashamed. I do want to say this: there is an old playground rule - You can say what you want to me or about me, but never talk about a person's mom. My relationship with my mom is loving but complicated, so we will leave it at that. It's the right thing to do.

I managed to get a ride with a friend of mine. She borrowed her mom's car to take me to the clinic. She dropped me off at the clinic entrance and said she would be back later to pick me up. I watched the car drive away... like a scared child watching their parent drive away on the first day of school. I wished I were still in the car. I was processed in, paid the amount that was requested, and sat to wait my turn. I examined the waiting room, to keep my mind off of things. It wasn't cared for... but it was a sterile room, beige color, drab, outdated and worn out like it had seen better days. I feel the same. It was quiet and somber. I was scared and nervous about what was getting ready to happen. Every muscle and nerve was trembling. Lost in my own racing thoughts, I felt so alone in this room full of women. Then a rebellious thought popped into my head. "How come I had to "find" someone to drive me... or come with me? Why do I have to do this alone and how come no one seems to care about me? I am not brave enough to tell someone I don't want to do this?

Would someone please ask me? Would I be brave enough to tell them the truth if they asked? What would happen to me if I did?" It changed nothing - I sat and I waited. I'd like to think I would've been brave, but I'll never know for sure.

I was startled from my thoughts as I was called to the back. I was in the exam procedure room trying to undress from my waist down but my legs were so shaky I had to lean against the exam table. As I lay down on the exam table, I was still wondering if I was doing the right thing. There was still time to change my mind. I couldn't get the sound out of my ears - the heartbeat from the ultrasound. Maybe it was just my own heartbeat, I don't know but I felt the heat in my face from my own shame.

In my mind I imagined jumping up and running out of that room and away from everyone and everything.

I looked at the picture of mountains, a waterfall with a rainbow. It was taped on the ceiling. What a joke but they meant well. It's supposed to be an emotional and psychological escape during the procedure. I wanted to crawl through it before we even got started. The only thing that held me there was what Heartache said. "If you want what I have and you want to start over you have to do this." I was trembling with the fear of the unknown. "Was it going to hurt?" I wondered. It's the first time I remember hearing a different kind of voice in my mind. It was a nasty voice. I tried not to pay much attention to that voice because there was so much happening. I was thinking about a lot of stuff and none of it was happy.

The doctor came in, he was an older man, and he looked a

little tired to me. He explained what was going to happen and then started the abortion. Halfway through the doctor said to me, "Someday you are going to be a great mother, just not to-day." I wanted to find some comfort in what he said to me as I lay there having an abortion. Maybe he could tell how sad I was. I was using every mental trick I ever knew to maintain my composure and not cry. I couldn't stop my tears as they rolled warmly down the sides of my face into my ears. My throat was so thick that I had a hard time swallowing it hurt as I pre-tended not to cry, and I worked really hard to keep my breath-ing steady.

"God, please forgive me. I feel so helpless. I have so much shame. I know there is no way that you can ever forgive me for what I am doing. I just had someone killed. Why didn't you save me? I asked you to save me. How come there is no one here who cares? How come I have to keep this to myself? Why will no one listen to me?" I spoke silently to my God.

While I was in recovery, I felt really cold and a sick sort of feeling. Like maybe I was going to vomit. I was on the edge of passing out. I remember closing my eyes and willing myself to stay present. I hear the buzzing in my ears. I don't feel good at all. I slowly opened my eyes and I looked around and realized that Heartache is right. I am a big baby. The room is full of nothing but women. There isn't a single man here except the doctor. I noticed that all of us women are not really looking at each other. Do they feel the same way I do? We look past each other. I mean, who wants to chat about it? That might be awkward. It's not like you can start the conversation with "So, why are you here?" I know why I don't want to make eye contact... it's because of what I just did - I had an abortion. It's because of what I did to get here, I got pregnant by accident. It's because of what I didn't do to stay out of here; I didn't take birth control. It's because I am here alone; I wasn't worth the time and effort for someone to come with me. It's shame. It's my fault. It's my entire fault. Heartache told me so.

There was a parallel reality missed by me, that day; we aren't damaged goods and we aren't outside of God's unfailing love, forgiveness, and compassion. And we can be whole again.

I was discharged. Just like that it was done. It was a very quiet car ride home. There was nothing that my girlfriend could say. Heartache called later that evening. "Hi", he said. "Hi." I replied. "So, did you go today?" "Yes." I answered. "Well, I went looking for a place for us to live and so and so..." I don't remember anything else he said. He wasn't calling to see if I was alright - he never asked. He was calling to see if I did what he wanted. Yes, I did. When he heard the answer he was looking for he went on like nothing had happened. Everything was back to normal for him. He happily chatted away. I couldn't wait to get off the phone that night. I made some excuse and got off the phone quickly. He told me he loved me and I said yeah you too and hung up the phone. He never said another word about it after that day. It was done for him. I wish it was that easy for me.

I didn't sleep most of the first night. My thoughts, like vultures, would circle around and around picking away at my peace. I'd replay the event over and over in my mind. What could I have done differently? What could I have said? What should I have done differently? The voice I had heard earlier was back this time to condemn me. That voice told me I was a coward, among many, many other things. It was easy to agree with that voice because I believe what I had done was wrong. I was tired and rest didn't come easily but eventually I dozed off just to wake up the next day to do it all over again.

I remember thinking for the first time, "Why not just give up? Why not give in?" That nasty voice was just standing on the edge of my mind waiting to torment me. Reminding me how stupid I was to get pregnant in the first place. I should be glad not to be stuck with a brat. I was lucky that Heartache still wanted to even marry me. If was willing to have sex with him what was keeping me from having sex with anybody? Why should Heartache trust me? I mean I really dodged a bullet. I could have been stuck with a kid and no husband then I would have been the loser that everyone already knows I am. When am I going to understand that I need to just do whatever Heartache says? Everyone knows you're a whore. Just keep your mouth shut and do as you're told and if you're lucky no one will ever find out. If I agreed with that nasty voice it would settle down a bit and it would only resurface when I needed a reminder to keep my head down and my mouth shut.

I've had a flood of thoughts. One thought has really stuck with me - and it frightens me. "What if Heartache really does change his mind?" What if he doesn't want to marry me now? I've never considered that before - it had now been introduced into my mind. I have no leverage. It took full root and I just can't bear to let that happen. That particular fear had taken me over. I was even more apprehensive about speaking up. I didn't want to risk losing him. I was losing the battle in my mind and spiraling. How was this happening? I thought my life had changed... that Heartache was my path to happiness.

The abortion was my early seventeenth birthday present; I quit school and got a GED trying to still convince myself I wasn't a total loser. I rounded it out with getting a job and going to work. I'm such a mess. It all happened so quickly. I worked every hour I could just trying to forget and trying to look ahead until it was time to move and get married. I couldn't face the people I knew because I didn't want to answer questions about what I had done. I felt like they were all talking about it because of all the voices talking about it in my head. I'm not healthy and Heartache seems to be happier than ever. I can't wait to get out of here and start over!

Taking A Moment:

After the abortion, I've come to realize how angry I was with God. I looked at God more like a genie in a bottle. When God didn't perform for me, I got mad. I suffered so many disappointments during that time and I had to blame someone, so I chose God. It was easier to blame God than to blame the person who could still hurt me. I started my journey with God thinking things would get easier but that wasn't true. I felt like He let me down and abandoned me. I suppose most children of divorce can have those tendencies... it's easy to transfer those feelings. Whatever the case, I felt abandoned.

God was with me. He was with me in the room speaking life to me through the doctor assuring me that I would make a good mother. I've come to believe it wasn't part of the plan for me to be a mother at sixteen. God was with me as my heart was breaking but I couldn't see it because I was confused and hurting. I believe God loves my baby perfectly in heaven as only He can. My hope is that we can have a conversation about mental, spiritual and emotional health surrounding abortion without judgment.

The time has finally come. I'm moving out and getting married. I'm putting everything else behind me. I'm moving on with the man I love.

CHAPTER 4

The Marriage

(THE MAN OF MY DREAMS)

Not everyday of our marriage was bad; I know that - I certainly thought that then. There were some well-intended and carefully manufactured moments of life that had, in contrast to other moments, "good" about them. And when you hunger for things to fit the image of "Happiness" you wanted so bad, for so long, you can rationalize almost any situation. The one true moment of joy I never needed to skew was the birth of my children. Nothing will ever top that. I'll always think of that time with a grateful heart and a smile that breaks the bondage of the bad. I wouldn't trade those moments for anything - a highlight among the craziness. But it took years and years of healing just to untangle the good from the cruel clutter. It all seemed to be so enmeshed. I wanted to begin this chapter with a positive outlook because, even now, I guess that's the story I wish I was telling, and well, it may be the last time I get to do that for a while... things start to get ugly fast. But I digress... like I said, there were periods of time that things seemed pretty good.

I'm getting married forever. That was my position, my heart and hope.

As I've pointed out - I wasn't the easiest child to raise. I wasn't perfect then and I'm not now. But I will say this; no matter how bad things got I always wanted to believe that everything was going to be fine because that's just who I am. I wanted to believe in dreams coming true and the fairytale wedding. Stuff every young girl (and boy) should have the opportunity to enjoy or at least experience in part, if not in whole. I wanted that so bad.

I'm going to see the man of my dreams today, a visit before we get married. I'm so excited to plan our future together. I can't wait to see him. I just love him so much. I've thought it through -okay, so we've had a rough couple of months but that's behind us and I can't wait to finish planning our wedding. I feel like all my dreams are getting ready to come true... just like I've imagined since I was a little girl.

I've arrived and just like that, we're off and running. We were in the car, on the way to what would become our new "home", and I was watching him. I really was studying him. He just kept talking endlessly about all the family I was getting ready to meet and how everything was set up for my arrival. Made me feel all the things I wanted to feel - a little special, I'll admit. "All set up for my arrival" - pinch me! Did anyone else hear that? After that I really wasn't paying much attention to all he was saying because I was just so happy to be in his presence and believing he was happy with me. That mattered a lot. That was enough for me - I was loved.

While I was visiting his hometown, we went and met with

the pastor of their family "church". I was really nervous and a little bit scared to be back inside a church. I hadn't been back inside one since the abortion. Inside my head I was thinking, "Can the pastor tell if I've had an abortion? Does God give him some kind of report?" I felt really guilty.

We were there for premarital counseling. I was surprised by how easy the tears came to me as the Pastor asked what would hurt us the most. I guess I hadn't done such a good job burying the touchy spots. I was quick to answer, "It would hurt not being loved for who I am." The Pastor pressed me for what I meant by that and I blurted, "Well, if I gained weight or looked different than I do now, I mean... I have struggled with my weight and it's a sensitive subject for me." I also told the pastor, "I don't like to be used." My gaze drifted over to the man of my dreams, he was looking down at his hands, fidgeting. A little hurt, I thought to myself, "Isn't this important? Have I done or said something wrong?" As I looked back to the Pastor, he reassured me that I would have nothing to worry about, that marriage is about more than looks. I really wasn't listening anymore because I was thinking about what the man of my dreams was doing. Then he looked up and smiled that smile that melts me. The man of my dreams agreed with the Pastor that I had nothing to worry about, that I looked just fine. Everything was okay again.

Living moment-to-moment waiting on his approval for me to be valuable...

I gazed upon him with blind admiration. I sat there waiting for his deep heart-felt answer to the same question I just answered. His answer surprised me, even embarrassed me. He stated clearly, "I don't want sex to be used as a weapon by her to get what she wants." He seemed to say it like he wanted the answer recorded, officially. I couldn't really wrap my mind around it. He had sex whenever he wanted it from me. He was always in control. His words stung. Up and out of my deepest hurts, and completely unable to stop it, I looked at him directly and said, "I haven't used it yet... I don't think you have anything to worry about." Yes, I said it. I can't believe I said it. Why did I say it? It was one of those times I wish I could have sucked the words back in and never said them.

The car ride back to the house was silent. I knew I had made him very, very mad. I know not to talk because it will only make it worse. I thought we were supposed to be honest, talk things out, not withhold from each other? Can't I be upset or offended too? Can't we at least argue, like healthy couples do? Some, any, form of communication would be better than this. Only silence. I don't know what to do to make it better. He dropped me off at his parents' house and left. "Where's he going?" His mother asked, "What happened?" My face red with embarrassment, I didn't answer I just shrugged went back to the bedroom and quietly closed the door until he returned. Self-possession, self-respect, self-assurance, self-confidence, self-worth, self-image, self-esteem, self-regard... SELF! Are all won and lost in moments like this. While I waited, he gained all the control. This was a tactic the man of my dreams used often. Yes, everyone argues and fights that's why it's difficult to explain to someone (that's not living with this kind of person) how methodical, debilitating and damaging it really is. How can you help someone to understand something you haven't been able to grip?

I'm going home today, and I am kind of relieved. I *think* things are okay - but that's the best I can ever do is guess. I don't really know for sure. We didn't talk about what happened. It was never spoken of again. He gets to decide that. Another thought to ramble around in my head and something else to obsess over.

> I want to scream but I know I can't because who's going to listen - what good will it do?

My thoughts don't stay settled anymore. I love him, I love him, I love him... I can't marry him. What am I doing? In haste, I called him today and called off the wedding. He told me I was being immature. I am immature. I'm seventeen years old. He hung up on me. I called back. He pretended to be his brother and assured me that everything I was feeling was normal. I don't understand why he had to pretend to be someone else... yet; I played along so he wouldn't hang up again. Mind games. Mind games. Mind games. By the end of the conversation the wedding was back on. What on earth am I doing?

Today when I was quiet, I heard God whisper to me "No, do not marry him." Maybe it's just an echo of my residual thoughts. No. This was different somehow, deeper. But I thought there was no way God would ask me to do that. Why would you ask me to do that God? You know what I've just gone through. You know what price I just paid. Yes, He did know - and clearly (though not to me at that time) that was the point - but I missed it. I'm invested and blind. God you know I'm desperate to be loved and willing to do anything for anyone who says they love me. That itself is sad. Please - He says he will love me. I stubbornly believe him. I have faith in him, the man of my dreams. God why are you making me question this? God loved and valued me more than I was willing to see or experience for myself - so, I pushed on.

Nothing is the way I imagined it would be. I can't really tell you exactly what I had imagined my wedding would be like, but I thought I was supposed to be a little more the center of attention than I am... just this one day. Upon my arrival, I entered the house and passed by all the wedding presents that sat on the dining table, opened and waiting for me. Petty, maybe; but should I have opened those gifts? The work was waiting for me to write the thank you notes. Oooh that got all over me, it irked me. Maybe that was just the teenager in me. It was as if someone, a family member or my husband to be was waiting, always waiting, with an explanation as to why I should not be upset by any of what was happening. They had a very unique talent for making the unreasonable sound reasonable. I always found myself agreeing whether I wanted to or not. I didn't know why?

It was a couple of days before the wedding and everything was just perfect. The family had taken care of every detail. I can't stand the way I sound, bitter and ungrateful, but I'm feeling a little overwhelmed. I feel like an outsider at my own wedding. I'm being told everything. Where to be and when, what to do - and while it may seem nice, it doesn't really feel nice. I feel like a puppet or a prop. I thought being a grown-up was going to be different, but it somehow feels a little worse. I am a little scared, and I feel very out of control. I wish some-one was here for me.

There is no turning back.

I wonder if the family is trying to overwhelm me on pur-pose. Are they trying to get me to change my mind? Is there a reason for doing this to me before I say I do? Maybe they don't think I'm good enough. Confusing new thoughts being introduced to the spin-cycle of my mind. I wasn't crazy - it just felt like it at times. In the end, it was likely none of that, they were simply being who they were. It was unimportant to in-clude me when they already knew what was best.

On my wedding day at the church I realized that I had con-trol over nothing. The bridesmaids, flowers, groomsmen, dec-orations, the ceremony, reception, cake all of it was different than what I had chosen. The only thing I had any control over was my dress, veil, and the artificial flowers I brought with me.

Yes, the wedding was nice. The way you would admire someone else's taste in decor. I guess I'm grateful, but I'm still kind of resentful. I'm really having a hard time trying to think that I'm feeling both but I am. I can't remember the brides-maids' names. They're his family. They are becoming my fam-ily. His groomsmen are his family. Everyone at the wedding is his family. They are becoming my family. There are so many of them. There are only two with me: my mother and my brother; the man who walked me down the aisle is an ex-fiancé of my mother. I put on a happy face. "It will be okay", I said to myself. It's my wedding. It's supposed to be a happy day. It will be okay. I'll get through it.

Because I was seventeen when I got married, my mother had to sign my marriage license - I wasn't of legal age. It wasn't until I had children of my own that I wondered how come it seemed so easy for my mother to sign it? I'm not going to judge her. I won't pretend to know what she was thinking. I had made up my mind that I was getting married. I was not an easy teenager. I imagine that she was probably relieved to transfer the responsibility to someone else.

After the service, we left for our honeymoon. Finally! We're alone. I thought to myself, I like it better when we're by ourselves... can we just always be by ourselves?

It wasn't too long after our return from the honeymoon before the honeymoon was over. "Why didn't you wave hi to Mr. [so and so]?", he says. "Honestly, I don't know Mr. [so and so]. Why should I wave to a complete stranger?" He quickly shot back, "Well you met him at the wedding!" "I met him a long with one hundred other people who are your family and friends. Do you honestly expect me to remember them all?" I replied and just looked at him dumbfounded. It was the second time I had seen him lose his temper (maybe a slight understatement) over something I thought was insignificant. The resulting hole in the wall next to my head was proof of his anger and a clear, unspoken, reminder that he may not choose to miss again. I never seem to understand what sets him off. I mean, yes, I knew what the circumstances were, but don't others just discuss it and move on? I'm not allowed to discuss it. As I've said, I wasn't told that, in so many words, I've come to learn it... like a child learns a look from a parent, a dog understands its master.

I'm learning my place.

The family isn't helping much. Am I just now noticing, or have they always been so judgmental and critical? I feel like I don't fit in too well. I've been trying. The more I try the less I fit. I feel awkward and out of place. So, I stay home alone a lot. It's lonely here. There's no one to talk to. It's unbearably hot here in the south; all I really do is sit and watch television, eat and smoke cigarettes. I've gained some weight and I'm more than a little nervous about that. No one has said anything. I know my insecurity is showing. It seems to be a big deal to everyone, how everything looks.

I guess today is the day my mother-in-law has decided to be concerned about my "image" masqueraded as my health; she gave me some diet books for my nineteenth birthday. The man of my dreams brought them home and told me that his mother sent them. In the birthday card my "concerned" mother-in-law told me it was my duty to lose weight. My face bright red, she hurt my feelings. I was so hurt I shredded that birthday card into a million tiny, little pieces and threw it in the trash. I didn't ask for her help. I don't understand why my husband isn't taking my side or even comforting me. He told me, "Quit over reacting" I explained, "I'm not, this was rude and none of her business and I'm not going up there for a while!" His responded with, "You aren't going to tell me to choose you over my parents!" I'm now crying and said, "I didn't ask you to choose!" I just wanted, what I always wanted, some reassurance of his love. He said, "Then you can just sit home." That particular part of my training backfired on him because I have no problem being by myself. I find myself sitting on the couch and crying a lot but eventually I wipe away my tears, accept my reality and shoved everything else aside as well as down deep. I chose this so I'm determined to damn well figure it out. I can see no other way out. So, we're marching ahead with building our life. He's working 2nd shift at one job, in a factory, and working part time at another job. I'm in community college. In our spare time, we fight - off and on.

The violence is escalating.

He's leaving bruises now, not to mention my spirit is being crushed; slowly and methodically each time we fight. The man of my dreams is breaking things he knows mean something to me - to taunt me. It's amusing to him. He's a Bully. What he's teaching me is not to get too attached to anything it's safer that way. I'm building walls around my heart and mind at a break-neck pace. Which is the perfect dance partner for my inner voice, "You deserve this you know... why not just give in? It would go so much easier if you would just give up and do whatever he wants" How much more can I do? "Whatever he wants" has no bounds - the more I give the more he takes. I wonder how far this will go? Is this my duty as a wife? I'm disappearing.

He's taking pieces of me I wasn't ready or prepared to give.

As I do my household chores, I watch him out of the corner of my eye or glance at him as I pass by. I know better than to get caught watching him too long and think to myself,

"What am I doing wrong? Why doesn't he trust me? How come he seems to hate me? What can I do to change his mind? What can I do to prove to him my love? How much harder can I work to show him?" I wish I understood why the man of my dreams is more suspicious lately. He always wants to know what I'm doing. Who am I talking to? Where am I? Like I have a secret life that he's not controlling. The only secret life I have is the inner thoughts I don't dare share - which he doesn't care to hear. I'm in community college and spend a majority of my time at school. I often wonder what he thinks I'm doing. He makes me feel guilty even when I know I have nothing to feel guilty about.

I love school. I get the rules of school. It makes sense. I'm working towards a goal and achieving it. I feel personal satisfaction again. Yes! This makes me happy! I'm too busy to be doing much of anything else. I can't escape him, even at school, because I'm constantly obsessing about what he's thinking. It's amazing I do as well as I do. I'm working hard; I so desperately want him to be impressed and happy with me.

I suppose in some ways I do live a double life. At school I appear to be happy, outgoing and personable - I feel like such a fraud. I think someone is going to find out I'm not what I present to be. I always must make sure no one knows or suspects anything "wrong" is happening at home, because I'm too embarrassed that I'm in this situation. I'm the picture of the perfect college student. Everything has to appear to be perfect.

I came to realize why I was even allowed to go to community college - it was an investment for him. If he put a little money in now, he could milk the cash cow later. This sounds harsh. It is harsh. There always has to be some angle of benefit for him. That's how it works. He could tell everyone how he "supported" me while I "got" to go to college. He could be the hero... and he played that role well for all to see. It's always about him. He saw me as a resource. It was never about what made me happy, it was about what more he could get out of me. I didn't have many skills other than I knew how to work hard (which he had seen when he met me) and he knew I was smart too (when I was in school A's came easily). So, by educating me a little (just enough - not enough to jeopardize his ego) and then putting me to work to earn my keep, I was a good return on his investment. I was just so happy and grateful to get to go to "college" I didn't even realize what he was doing to me.

I'm about half way through community college; I'm starting to see the finish line and I just found out that I am pregnant. I am excited; but not for long. I lost that pregnancy. I miscarried. I am devastated and feel like maybe God is punishing me for the abortion. I'm also afraid that if I can't have a baby that I would be considered damaged goods. I could be thrown away for not being perfect.

Fast forward a couple of years and two children later...

He's started drinking and is coming home really late, early morning hours, regularly. When he comes in he wakes me up. He's in my face with his drunken breath, talking about all kinds of irrational, random stuff. Big dreams and crazy plans all these "people" he's met (at the bar) are telling him. I've reached my breaking point. I told him to get out. I am serious. He raged, I'm afraid but I hold my ground. I grew up in an alcoholic household and my children simply were not going to. I'm sure of that. I gave him an ultimatum. I told him, "You either stop drinking or don't come back. I don't care where you go just don't come back here until you stop!" He tried to wheedle, he tried to justify but for once I wasn't having it. I stuck my heels in the dirt, good or bad I wasn't going to budge. I have no idea how I'm going to make it but I am done with his drinking.

He's been gone for several days. He sent his family over to "talk to me". The salesman went all over town selling his story about me throwing him out. How unfair I was to him. How was he going to live without his children? Sob, sob, sob... it's an old story... he was politicking. The part that always gets left out of his story is what he's like when he's drunk at home. The man of my dreams is a living nightmare. He uses his drunkenness to get what he wants.

He knows that I'll do anything to keep the kids out of it.

He makes his demands and threatens to get loud if he doesn't get his way. He would rather have me agreeable but whatever works. He forces himself on me without shame or dignity. I'm his property, his investment, and his nothing. The smell of the alcohol on his breath and oozing out of his skin feels like rape to me but I think, "How can it be if I'm married to him?" Is this his right? I know I hate him for it.

I don't fight back - my daughters are in the next room sleeping. You become numb or hate yourself. I chose numb.

Agreeing with the man of my dreams makes it go quicker and he's sleeping it off before we both know it. Around town he's a likeable kind of guy. He's everybody's friend and he will do anything for you - that kind of guy. It was real easy for everyone to give me a hard time and for people to tell me "Aww just give him another chance. Everyone makes their share of mistakes." If only they knew but I wasn't going tell them. He would always spin it and make sure they'd never believe me anyway. I don't know how he does it but he always does. Manipulation was like breathing for the man of my dreams. I'm no Psychiatrist (as I'm sure you've figured out), and I take mental health issues very seriously. I would never assume a diagnosis or label someone - that would be reckless and unqualified. However, I have lived long enough on this earth to know - a narcissist can have a convincing smile... as easily as anyone else.

He sobered up and came over and is trying to convince me that he isn't going to drink again. I am stubbornly awaiting some sign that he is finished with the drinking. I don't really believe him, but I listened to what he has to say. Like so many times before, those voices were always whispering in my ear to just believe him. This time I was stalling. What I failed to realize, buried under my own fears, was that I genuinely had my own power and was wielding it during this short period of time.

While I've been waiting for my answer, out on the back deck of the trailer, I was watching the children play and I had a vision. I knew that I would let him back in but I also knew that I would leave one day. I never told anyone what I saw in my mind's eye that day. The picture was perfectly clear to me.

I was absolutely certain and I had absolute peace. It was the strangest sensation. I knew it was God talking to me. I had felt that feeling before. It was startling. I knew I could make it work until I was forty. I didn't know how but I knew I would. My two children would be grown and I could go. He returned home. Somehow for me, I felt I could make it knowing that my "sentence" would someday come to an end. In a twisted way I saw it as a "win-win."

> Year after year... nothing seems to change, one foot in front of the other. Time is just passing.

I encourage him to have his hobbies. It doesn't matter whether I encourage him to do anything or not because if he wants to do something he just does it. I never argue against it. That's who he is. I'm just grateful for whatever would take him away from the house. He goes off and dirt bikes or whatever he does. I would watch him as he packs all his gear into the truck and load his bike excitedly talking about all he was going to get to go do, like a little kid. I had grown to appreciate his indifference because it gave me freedom to do a little of what I wanted. He has a few friends he's gone with all day - I'm fine with that. The trips would sometimes go over a weekend; they'd go off into the woods around the house we lived. Peace would reign at home for a few hours.

After all these years I would find myself looking at him and still thinking to myself, "Will I ever get in? Will I ever deserve your love or loyalty?" Nothing had changed on the family front - I still felt like an outcast and never felt that I was able to live up to anyone's expectations. I would over hear them talking. I was always a good source for their snickers. My house was never clean enough, I was too fat, and too stupid. I was constantly made aware of my shortcomings. I was still trying to "fit in" but usually found myself being silent and just listening. I often wondered how come the others that married in seemed to have no problem fitting in. Is it just me? Are they playing the same "all is well" game we all played? I was missing something but that wasn't a news flash - that was the norm. How come after all these years I still don't get it? It makes a person want to question everything. Am I really what they say about me?

I was already catering to him on many levels. In an effort to be more I would make him a cup of coffee and delivered it to his bedside every single morning. The man of my dreams would wake up to a hot cup of Joe, just the way he liked it, to show him that I love him. In response he has accused me of trying to poison him with that coffee love offering - yet I still do it with the hopes that someday he can receive it with the love that I do it. Yes, that is crazy. But it's all I know to do. All I've ever known to do. I've thought that perhaps no one has ever really just loved him and that's why I try so hard. Sometime I get a little pious and think when my love cracks him... he'll see and then he'll be so grateful that I didn't quit on him. Then he'll let me in. I'll have what I've wanted all these years and all this sacrifice will be worth it. It's been one of my daydream fuels to keep me going.

The years are passing I find myself the well-trained juggler. My main job is to constantly make sure that every little detail of everything, everyday is okay for the man of my dreams. Anything will set him off. So, I work tirelessly to think ahead

- to cut off any potential problems at the pass. I work hard to keep the façade of perfection for him. I keep shoving my feelings aside or down or anywhere there's still a space to shove them. I'm running out of room and at times I feel like I can't breathe. Yet I keep moving. I think I'm staying one step ahead of everything that's going on; and then I realize I am just chasing my tail because it is never enough.

He has a deeper psychological hold on me than I'm willing to admit.

Something's got to change. Now in my mid-thirties, my children are entering middle school and high school and things... they just can't go on the way they are. Why won't I acknowledge it's abusive? What's wrong with me that I stay? Not long now - my vision of leaving is still as clear as my need for him to accept me and let me in. I'm a conflicted mess. I can't take it. He knows, he always knows when it's story time. The stories he tells me are so believable. His stories were always believable. He came home one day and, "I ran into them while on a job!", he said. Trust him, I was going to "love them", he said. He was adding a new distraction. I was ready for anything. Change was good!

CHAPTER 5

Children

(THE MAN OF MY CHILDREN)

Today is a great day - amazing news! I'm pregnant again and this time the pregnancy is for keeps. The months are going by quick. I think maybe things are changing. I hope things are changing. The man of my children hasn't hurt me while I am pregnant. Oh sure, he still gets in my face and yells but nothing physical. I can handle the yelling. I've become immune to the yelling. It doesn't really bother me that much anymore. At least that is what I tell myself. I think he's somewhat relieved that I'm pregnant it tethers me to him. If I had graduated from college, and hadn't been pregnant, there'd be a chance I would've left. I don't think he liked those odds - he protected his investment.

He's happy I'm pregnant and he wants a son. I am praying for a daughter. It is my opinion that he doesn't deserve a son. I'm praying God will honor my prayers. I think by having a daughter I'll have much more influence over her life than he will. He's been on a spending spree; he's been out buying everything imaginable for the baby. It's been nice to see he's excited. At least maybe he'll care more for the baby than he has for me. I have great hopes that this baby means we'll be our own family and separate from "the family".

I gave birth to a baby girl today and she is perfect in every way.

It didn't seem to matter to him that she was a she. He was happy. I was back in his good graces again. I was basking in his glow. It felt good. Things were looking up. I just graduated from community college, a double degree with academic honors, my six-week-old daughter present, and all by the age of twenty. I was offered a full scholarship to a four-year college but that was a threat to the man of my children and I was forbid to go. I was just offered a dream of mine on a silver platter. His answer was a screaming, spit flying "No!" "No wife of mine is going to a black state college, scholarship or no scholarship." I just wanted to hate him. I'm bewildered and feeling oppressed. I wondered if this would be a harbinger of what my children would have to look forward to?

It's hard for me to believe I was so excited one second and so demoralized the next. I honestly believed that he would be happy for me. I thought things were changing. That he would recognize his wife's achievement and be proud... maybe even tell his family. His mother and mine came to the graduation but while most families would see this as a reason to celebrate, a victory in life. I just wanted--- well, it didn't matter. The man of my children was incapable of seeing someone else's wants. Again, managing his interests. My happiness was never a part of the game plan. I worked so hard and the scholarship was evidence of that. I stood there looking at him and wondering who in the hell had I married? How come I didn't know these things about him? I said nothing. I always said nothing. I cried bitter tears when I was alone. I just kept pushing it down. I have my daughter. Thank you God for my daughter.

The reality of raising my child makes me feel a new deepened sense of responsibility and purpose. I had tapped a new well of love and was willing to do whatever it took to keep her safe. I was determined to create a home with both of her parents... even if the man of my dreams had shown his hand. I made a decision, a new sort of covenant, that if I couldn't have the fairytale marriage then she was going to have a fairytale life. She was going to grow up with both parents at home.

Three months later I'm pregnant again and the following year I have another beautiful baby girl. I am working at a job and hating every minute of it. I want to be home raising my children but the man of my children wants me working, "chip in", to bring home money and benefits. I have never had a problem doing my part. He works too - he does physical labor and he puts in some long hours. I would be reminded that he didn't want *me* to get "Too distracted." I actually snort out loud laughing when I think about that statement. He wanted to make sure I was busy... a busy mind can't wonder. Who's got time to be distracted? We both work hard the difference is, when I get home, I'm spending time with and raising my two children, I'm taking care of the home and I'm taking care of him. I often find myself watching him as he does what he wants as I am busy doing everything else. Who is taking care of me?

I was now in my mid-twenties; I had my third child; another perfect little girl. Thank you God for another healthy baby girl. The man of my children really connected to her. His relationship with her was... different. Things were different for her. She was conceived and born after he had been let back into the house. He referred to her as his "Second chance kid." He bonded with her in a way he didn't with the first two. It was a little sad and confusing; how could he not bond with all of his children? I didn't want them to feel less loved. She had a much stronger resemblance to him and his side of the family then our other two daughters. He loved that. It was like looking in a mirror. As time went on it became apparent, and yes it may seem crazy but, when he looked at her, he was looking at himself. He bonded with an image of himself. If only I were making this up.

While I was on maternity leave with my last daughter; my desire to be with them grew as well as the desire to have more children. When I approached my husband with what I wanted, I was met with a resounding, "No!"

"Why? You come from a large family... I don't understand." His response was, "That's exactly why! The answer is no..." After that the talk of getting "fixed" became a sore subject. I had to wait one year after my last child to get "fixed" and the subject of him getting fixed was completely off the table. When the year had passed, the doctor appointment was scheduled. Now where I lived, if you were married, your husband had to approve the sterilization surgery. Yes, that's the way it was. Like a good wife, I went in and got the procedure done. At age twenty-six, I would never be able to have children ever again.

My children are growing fast and with the exception of the

youngest, he's fairly distant and hands off with the older two. He still rages through at times wanting to be the disciplinarian. His method is to berate and belittle them - I still don't know what sets him off. It's a trigger that's only known in his mind. At other times he would spend hours lecturing them. Sometimes I thought that perhaps he felt guilty and somehow "talking them to death" would fix things. It never did. It just wore them down. He'll blame me and point out some shortcoming in me as a wife or mother. I gladly take it if it means they don't have to. He always has to be right even if he doesn't know what's going on. Some things never change they just continue on in different forms. I do my level best to keep quiet about things going on in the children's lives and let things go or try to handle them myself unless I have no choice but to say something to him. Maybe that was wrong but I don't think so. I had no real reason to trust him when it came to the children-like I said, he was mostly disinterested unless it directly affected him or his image. The man of my children knows that's one time I will fight. He doesn't seem that interested in playing with his children. He doesn't change diapers to speak of, he doesn't do doctor appointments, he doesn't go to school functions or do homework other than the "big events" like graduations or awards. The events where he can take credit for the amazing children he has. I don't think he realizes, even to this day, how amazing his children are. He has no patience for the mundane business of raising children. The repetition that is often necessary in training children is maddening for him. My heart breaks for my children. I pray God's protection over their hearts and minds that they don't feel rejection by their father.

While the children were in elementary school I ended up working with him at his business. I'd finally left working in the corporate world. It wasn't easy for me to work with him but it did give me what I wanted which was more time with my children. They were with me as much as they could be. We settled into a routine of life. I learned not to expect much, to just work and get my enjoyment from my children. Let him do what he wanted.

Before my children were born, I could not bear to drag myself to the family church. I guess for me it was quiet rebellion. It was presented as the only option. There was no discussion. As I look back I wonder why I didn't just go somewhere else to church. I've come to believe it was what I told myself, a misinformed, misguided sense of what marriage is. I thought if I was going to talk to God, I was going to talk to him on my terms on my couch and not in that place called church. I wasn't really talking to God much except when I was in absolute crisis. Even when I was in crisis, I was just yelling at Him, blaming him and accusing him. Then I would be silent with Him. I was treating Him more like the absent father or abusive husband than the loving, sovereign God He is. He patiently let me get it all out of my system.

My father told me when I was a teenager that he felt it was his job to expose me to religion or spiritual things until I was old enough to make my own choices. It was my father's words that came up in my mind repeatedly until I made the decision to pick up where I left off with a "new improved" relationship with God when my children were preschool. I resigned myself to the fact it was going to happen at the family church. The contribution to the decision from the man of my children, was, "If it was good enough for me, it's good enough for them." That was it. Somehow, I knew it would be okay, I guess kind of like my Dad knew I would be okay. So, I decided that I was going to play an integral part and became their teacher. It made perfect sense to me. I could participate in what they learned. I never had to worry about interference by their father because there was no way he was every going to teach-that was a woman's job. I wanted to give my children something to lean into when times get tough. There was nothing easy about the household they were growing up in. I prayed for God to protect their hearts and minds. I wanted them to be able to find some peace. I wanted to show them that shelter can exist for them from the chaos that swirls around them. I hoped I could show them or teach them about real love - the "lay down your life" kind of Jesus love. I wanted them to see real love does exist in humanity and that real love is free. The seeds of both can be found within us. So I started rebuilding that relationship with God and teaching my children about Him.

I'd take the children to the movies or the pool or they would have friends over. The house would become a place where all the kids would come and play or watch television. When he was home and the children were there it would be safe from his rage and antics. He mostly just stayed away, doing his own thing. Things always had to appear perfect, so I arranged for our house be where everyone wanted to be. I was becoming good at the game he put in place. I totally took advantage of it for as long as I could. Things were fine for a while... as long as the children were dependent on me for rides and needed me to pick up friends or drop friends off. I had a pretty firm rule that my children's friends stayed with us. My children didn't really get the chance to spend the night away from home, unless it was his family, until they were in late middle school and high school. As they grew, and became more independent, things were changing again. But it's supposed to change for them; children are supposed to grow up and become independent - stretch their wings and fly. I certainly want that for them. But it truly was an emotional and psychological battle for me, as it meant my defense system was failing again. Don't get me wrong, I don't mean that in the sense that I'd ever place my children in harms way - my life before theirs. He knew that. My children were my purpose; but they were also my escape and protection from him. I know how that sounds - but I'm being honest. I don't think they ever knew... but I struggled with it. They had their friends, fun, they played and lived like (as close to what I imagined) "normal" children in a healthy family lived like. I kept my children as safe as I knew how - but in truth it was me that felt safe because of them. I love to look back on those times because it gives me some satisfaction in knowing that I gave that to them.

From the outside looking in, we looked like the picture-perfect family. We had all the trappings of the American dream: the house, the cars, the toys, the clothes. I was glad that they had those things it made the scales feel balanced or was a guilt offering - it kind of teetered between the two. Inside that home, the accusations he made were growing wilder by the day. I wanted to trust him but knew better. Our surroundings started to feel more dangerous again because the children were older and more willing to stand up to him. I felt like they really didn't understand the fire they were playing with because of the level of sheltering I had done for them. All of it was scaring me in new ways. I am running out of ways to manage the children and him.

I don't like talking about motherhood and being an abused woman/wife. For me, it feels like we're talking about two different people. As a mother I felt mostly whole. I was driven to see that my children were healthy, happy and okay. I would do anything for them, well, until I couldn't. It's messy. That's when the abused wife kicks in. The scale tipped out of proportion internally for me and even though I still wanted to be that mother, there were times I just couldn't be. There were times toward the end of my marriage that I reacted to my circumstances and then tried to do damage control with my children. I was so focused on their health and wellbeing, for so much of their lives. It seemed like I had been a good "manager" of what was happening to and around my children. Now that my children are adults, sadly, I can see that in some ways my management failed. The places that are whole and undamaged in my children I give sole credit to God above. Yes, I absolutely love my children. I have and always will love my children but God loves them more. As much as I tried, the circumstances of their lives, with regard to their father, our marriage, their family life and me - it was ultimately God that protected their mind, will and emotions.

My children were bold and surprisingly had very little fear of the man of my children. That's not to say he could not hurt them. He did. He was using the same games and tricks on them the older they got. The name calling, the belittling remarks. He would somehow manage to swirl us all together.

This may sound strange but at times I often thought he would confuse them with me. It was mainly the older two that took the brunt of his nastiness. I just don't understand how a father could be jealous of his own children, to the point of wanting to destroy them and their psyche. I would step in between them every chance I got. I would spend whatever time necessary working tirelessly to undo the damage he would cause.

My eldest daughter - I smile now thinking about her bravery at such a young age. She stepped out and decided she wasn't going to live like we were. She made it happen and never came back. We became a visually divided family. The oldest had left, the youngest was fully entrenched with her father and the middle daughter and I were somewhere in the middle.

The man of my children had told me, I could not have any contact with my eldest daughter. None of us were allowed. I could not see her, help or support her in any way. Her perceived betrayal of Him was not tolerated in the slightest. How rich given his betrayal of her was so profound. It did what it was supposed to do though; it made the rest of us fall back into line - at least for a while.

CHAPTER 6

The Friend, The Traitor, The Straw

(DECEIVER)

My idea of a friend is someone you can spend time laughing with, talk about anything with - and never run out of stuff to say. They're a person you share private thoughts with, even your deep dark thoughts... someone you can trust with no judgment. This kind of friend has your back and is with you; we'll both share in our burdens and our joys... and even a little bit of juicy gossip. Loyalty isn't an option. That's what I wanted. We should all have this... shouldn't we?

Sixteen years into my marriage and my husband has decided to do something he's never done. He set up a date. Not just any date though, it was a double date with Deedee and her husband Al. And he was really looking forward to the dinner. Excited like a child on Christmas Eve, he filled me in on the "backstory". He told me every detail about the mad crush he had on Deedee in middle school, how he and his cousin had competed for her attention. She was apparently drool-worthy. During high school he had tried repeatedly to gain her affections. He "envied" her husband for having "won" her and how "she got away". This type of in-my-face conversation was his way of making me feel small, ugly, and insignificant. More mental warfare - it's hard to explain to people, unless they live it day in and day out. It takes its toll, if you let it. As I distanced myself mentally in that moment - I remembered my first mad crush. I didn't share it with him because it was a long time ago and I didn't want to hurt his feelings or make him feel... well, the way I do in this moment. Actually, I thought it was kind of humorous how animated he was in retelling this story. Other than that, I didn't really put much thought into what he was saying because all his stories were, hmm, "Dramatic" isn't the word I'm looking for - sensationalized - yeah that's more accurate. To me, this one was no different. I mean high school was a long time ago and we were all very married now, and life goes on, for most of us anyway.

As it would happen, we had a good time at dinner. She was outgoing and friendly. She was blonde, petite, buxom, cute, flirty and extremely feminine-pretty much the exact opposite of me. Even saying all that, it was easy for me to like her. That's me though; I find common ground with people quite easily. Her husband was personable too. He had been hurt in an accident and had some physical limitations but he more than made up for that with his wit and kindness. I left dinner that night thinking that this could be a good thing and I definitely looked forward to doing more things with them as a couple. But I always left dinners with other people feeling that way. I like people. I enjoyed the opportunity of outside human connection. We exchanged phone numbers and made arrangements to talk again soon.

The thing I think I liked best about this new potential friend - she was from the area but not part of the family. As an early 30 something, I felt like I had been released out of friend jail because my husband liked Deedee and Al. He arranged the "dinner date" so all systems were go. You know, I'd done my time and now I get a friend my husband liked... this could be good? A friendship he encouraged.

I never thought for a second that I could be set up...

Seems I never do. Was it the years of mental conditioning or just my blind optimism? My belief in and love for my Deceiver was always my Achilles heel. Until Deedee, every friendship I formed on my own he never liked. He would always (which is not an exaggeration) discourage the friendship. He would start out saying "Sure, they're nice. I had a pretty good time." But by the second invite, he would start with, "You know, I really didn't like the way they said [such and such] or the way they did [this or that]..." The excuses were made and that would be the end of it. I never had a say. To finally have an "approved friend", well this was a whole new experience for me. I was excited. I was a fool.

I started working out, trying to get my act together, and not too long after Deedee joined me. The Deceiver suggested it. It was just the two of us. I enjoyed her company and the time spent talking with a woman. She encouraged me to make changes to become more feminine. They were things that I was interested in. Some of the things we discussed I knew absolutely nothing about; I'm a little embarrassed to say. I was fascinated that women did some of these "things" or wore some of these "things". For example, we had an entire conversation on the treadmill one night about thong underwear. What? I heard about them and thought they were utterly ridiculous. I mean who wants that up their butt? But she went on to explain, "No, they are quite comfortable once you get used to them and then you don't have any panty lines." I just laughed and laughed. I said, "Really? They don't get wedged in there like string on a yoyo?" She laughed and urged me to give them a try. I told her I would think about it. It was conversations like those that made feel, maybe for the first time, like I fit in. I didn't feel judged, just accepted for who I was - I was ok.

I would share with her things that interested me, like whatever I was reading or "hippy things" as she would call them and then she would laugh. I gave her some natural medicine advice for some skin problems she had, and she took the advice and it helped her. She was impressed and thankful. This to me is what friendship is, give and take. I did have something to give. To be friends with Deedee felt redemptive, in a way. She represented the "cool people" I went to school with or I saw around me in my adult life. The people I never quite felt like I fit in with and here she is... she's my friend. Somehow my friendship with her made me feel I wasn't the loser I felt I was (most of) the rest of the time. I really valued my friendship with Deedee. We laughed with each other and at each other, not in a mean way. It was fascinating that we could be friends but not share much in common - other than we wanted to be friends.

After occasional double dates we started including the kids with trips to the lake, boating and hanging out. Al was very good to my children. He spent time with them. He & Deedee had no children of their own and so Al, in particular, really enjoyed the time he had with them. He and his nephews taught my children and me how to waterski, kneeboard and wakeboard. Since Al had his limitations, he drove the boat and cheered us all on. He was such an excellent teacher. The children really liked him. I liked him. I really enjoyed being with them; they made things more meaningful. It was good clean fun. I had the opportunity to laugh with my children. I felt like that didn't happen near enough. I was happy that my pre-teen and teenage children wanted to spend time with me, and that made me feel a level of safety. I found myself letting my guard down and really enjoying the relationship.

Our lives were busy. We were becoming more entwined and we started spending more and more time together. It was a slow creep into our lives that I welcomed. We started eating out together just about every night of the week, after Deedee and I worked out. We stopped doing things as an independent family. Where we went, they went. I talked to Deedee about everything. I shared my insecurities and frustrations about my marriage because I trusted Deedee. She shared too. She told me about her marriage and how she felt suffocated by the neediness of her husband since he got hurt. We shared a lot as we walked all those evenings together. We encouraged one another. I thought to myself how God has blessed me with this friendship. It was the perfect transition. My safety net was being re-established through Deedee and Al. My husband's focus was not so much on the children or me but on our new-found friendship.

It seemed like things were going to be okay.

Then the presents started. Deceiver gave me and Deedee money to go treat ourselves with things like jewelry, pedicures, shopping. He was only that generous if Deedee was present. He talked so sweetly to her. He just doted on her and cared for her in ways he had never done for me. A few times I asked him, "Why do you do all these nice things for Deedee?" I would always stop short of asking him "And why not for me." His answer (to begin with) was, "Well, I feel a little sorry for her. I mean look at her husband. She has it so hard with him hurt like he is, and she still stays married to him. She deserves to be treated to nice things. She deserves some happiness. I am going to make sure to give it to her." His words stung. He defiantly said, "Do you have a problem with it? Look at what you have! Are you going to be selfish?" I knew not to take the bait, and of course replied, "No." He was going to do what he wanted and there was nothing I could do about it. Manipulated again. He treated my response like it was a form of permission. As if he needed it. This seemed to be a crossroads for him. It was his way of inching toward what he wanted all along. His self-seeking nature would have what it wanted - no matter who it hurt. I wasn't even factored into the equation. He started taking Deedee out to lunch, just the two of them. He would *tell* me he was going to do it - "out of respect" for me, he said.

The Deceiver had to poison everything.

He thought I was stupid. And why not - we teach the

predator how to prey. I was, in his eyes, too naïve to understand his crafty and intelligent ways. I had let him do this to me for so long. Then one day I woke up and looked around. I realized that my husband was talking with Deedee more often than he was before. He started showing up to the gym and working out with us. I started paying attention to what he was saying. He would flirt with her openly, in front of me. He became, occasionally, a little too touchy feely, something that would have raised the roof had the situation been reversed. At first, I tried to dismiss it but when it continued, I started to worry. He never tried to hide it from me. He called her several times a day and would never go to bed at night without speaking with her. I would sit on the couch next to him (in the recliner) as he talked baby talk to her and spoke sweet nothings. Then in that same sickening, sweet voice that he used to use on me, he would say, "goooood niiiighhht... no you hang up".

He waited for her to hang up... I waited for it to end.

Yes, that makes me sound jealous because I was. It had been years since I had heard that kind of talk. To hear it as a third party, at this point, just ate away at me with envy. Why her? Why not me?

I had scheduled some minor sinus surgery and was unable to attend an open house, at the school, with one of my children who were now entering middle school. The part that really killed me, hurt my heart was that Deedee was the one who went in my place. That was unacceptable for me on two levels; one, I was not the kind of Mom that ever allowed anyone to parent my children. Two this felt like another example of her trying to replace me. And when it came to my children - that, I assure you was never going to happen. Before the surgery we decided we were all going to go out - it was my turn to "pick the restaurant". When I chose, my husband checked in with Deedee to see if she was good with my selection. He was almost badgering Deedee to make sure that she was okay. I just reiterated my choice until all agreed that's where we were going. I was furious. Something inside me snapped. I felt like a three-year-old getting ready to throw a temper tantrum. The children were out visiting friends and staying the night elsewhere. When we got home that night the fight was on!

It was my turn...

For this one moment I was not going to let it go. He wanted to take everything from me. I absolutely blew my top and confronted the Deceiver with everything I had. I interrogated him. I asked question after question, trying to trip him up with what he was saying. Liar! User! Deceiver! He deserved everything he was getting. I was screaming, crying, accusing, questioning... like I had never done before. My face was red-hot with what I knew was coming. I followed him all over the house - tracking him. My anger and hurt gave me courage. I did a lot of screaming in my head too, not sure what came out and what stayed in. But it was bad. She's my friend - you're my husband! How could you do this to me? [Silly question. I know. But when you're beside yourself you're entitled to ask (or think) stupid questions]. He specialized in robbing my joy, took pleasure in seeing me wounded. He kept trying to escape me, but I wasn't done, not even close. He tried going to bed, not gonna happen - no sleep! Not this time. I kept after him until, until...

It was his turn...

He unleashed liked a roaring lion. "Yes!" He roared, "I love Deedee! I've loved her since high school!" I remember the spit flying from the Deceiver's mouth, as much as, the stab of his words. "She's my heart's desire and she does things to me that you will never do! She has a special place in my heart that you will never have!" It was his turn to rage and shove. He told me every single defect he saw in me and why Deedee was so much better. He warned me, "You better watch your step...you do anything, to treat Deedee differently or you try to end your friendship with Deedee I will make sure your life is a living hell." Then with ice and dead calm in his voice he said, "You are not allowed to end this friendship, you will still workout daily together, we will still do everything that we have done, or you will pay the price." I knew he meant it. My life was already a living hell, a hidden hell but hell, nonetheless. How much worse could he make it? I remember thinking I didn't want to find out.

How do you wrap your brain around a "life" like that? I had put up with many things but this? What he, in effect, told me to do... was play a role whereby my feelings and dignity don't count - a piece of bait to lure the love of his life into his twisted scheme. This was bigger and more overwhelming than my ability to cope. Was I human to him? When this plays itself out will I still feel human or have any self-resect left?

Two days later I went to see Deedee at work and broke

down as I was telling her what my husband had told me. Deedee cried. I stood there and watched. I didn't try to comfort her. I don't really understand why Deedee cried. I remember thinking, "Why are you crying? He loves you. He dotes on you. He treats you like a queen but I'm his wife. Why aren't you comforting me?" I wanted to believe she was crying about our friendship being forever changed. And our "friendship" was changed because after that day I looked at her not as a friend but an adversary, a traitor. I believe she was crying because she had been confronted with her treachery. I also believe that she definitively switched sides that day. If the cat was out of the bag, why not be honest about whom you were batting for? Not satisfied, I went to Al and again, I broke down crying, telling him what had happened and asking him to "please help me". Al said not to worry, it was just a mid-life crisis and it would pass. He wasn't worried about it and neither should I. I've often wondered about Al and why he said what he said. Part of me thinks that perhaps he felt a little trapped and deficient too, because of his injury. That perhaps Al had made some sort of peace with what his marriage would or wouldn't be. I had asked them both to back away from us. The two that would have been able to help me didn't. The Deceiver made it virtually impossible for any of us to slowly withdraw from one another. If anything, it made him more diligent in pursuing the Traitor - a way to punish me.

I went in for the sinus surgery. I prayed for the first time not to wake up - that the anesthesia would kill me. I wrote a letter to him and told him I was sorry for not being the wife he wanted, that if I woke up I would work harder at being a better wife but maybe it would be better if I never did [exhibit "A" as to my state of mind and clarity of thought]. Before I went under for surgery he came in and kissed me deeply, almost in a vulgar obscene way, and said not to worry everything was fine. My heart wanted it to be real, but my mind knew it wasn't. It was just another cruel manipulation to make himself feel better. I think it was his vain attempt to absolve himself from any responsibility for my mental state. You know, "just in case" anything did go wrong. When I woke up in recovery, I started crying, and I heard the voices in my head laughing. In desperation, I cried out to God and asked Him why? I heard nothing but laughter. I was bereft. I had lived to fight another day whether I wanted to or not.

Yet, I continued to stand by and let things unfold. I did nothing to stop it or even try to stop it. I was trying to live a dual life and it was taking its toll on me. I remember asking him if he wanted to sleep with both of us. [Yes, I actually asked him that]. I thought I was prepared to share him instead of lose him. He said, "I know you couldn't handle it." I felt rejected even in my offer of depravity. His answer proved it was definitely on his mind... if he hadn't already acted on it. He's right though I couldn't have handled it.

I was getting a lot of spiritual miles in - running to and from God at the same time. I was reading every Christian self-help book related to marriage, being a good wife doing, praying, and studying. Looking for reassurance, and not wanting to leave any stone unturned, I also sought the help of psychics and tarot, witchcraft and even casting spells (I will make you love me through this spell sort of thing). If someone had told me not showering would have saved my marriage, I would have stunk for the cause. You name it and I tried it. I so desperately wanted to save my marriage. I so desperately wanted to be loved.

And so, we vacationed with them. We ate with them. The Traitor came by our house every day. Our conversations and plans were centered on the Traitor and Al. Mainly the Traitor, but Al would be thrown in occasionally so as to not be so obvious. Deference was paid to the Traitor.

I would run back into the land of denial.

I would try to convince myself that I was just imagining things. It was my insecurities. The nonstop worrying and stressing myself out had one positive effect - I lost a lot of weight fast. Too fast as a matter of fact I lost like almost sixty pounds in forty-five days. I started trying to turn myself into a Deedee lookalike. I dyed my hair blonde and started to wear more makeup than I had my whole life. I wore red painted, artificial fingernails and jewelry. I dressed up more than I had in a long time. If you had asked me at the time, I would have denied it. I changed my taste in ways to match hers. I've looked back at those pictures. I see nothing but a shell -knowing that "I", the real me, was trying to disappear behind a veneer of her.

I was a complete fraud... but it seemed better than not existing at all.

As I look back now, I can understand (understatement) why my children were worried. My oldest that was in high school, confronted me about the Traitor and what was so obvious to them. But I would just brush it off. She yelled, "Mom! What's wrong with you? Can't you see what Dad is doing? He picks Deedee over you ALL THE TIME? Why don't you do SOMETHING? I DON'T UNDERSTAND WHAT'S WRONG WITH YOU?! WHY DON'T YOU MAKE THEM STOP?" I found myself using the Deceiver's script and saying, "You have this all wrong sweetie, they are just friends, and nothing is going on. Don't you trust me?" I just kept saying the same thing over and over until she stopped. I went downstairs, quietly closed the bathroom door and looked myself in the mirror and said, "You are a liar. You just lied to your child. You ought to be ashamed of yourself." I hung my head, asked God to forgive me and to somehow make everything okay. I just didn't know what else to do. At this point I was so immersed in the delusion I saw nothing clearly. I was lost.

I would reassure my children by making some lame excuse. "No one's going anywhere" and "The best way to torture your dad is to stay married to him." I wasn't willing to openly admit to anything. It simply didn't fit the life narrative I had created in my mind for my children. They didn't believe it and that was okay, it was my delusion.

To understand clearly, I felt like I was being body-snatched in some sort of nightmare where I was helpless to respond or fight back. Right before my very eyes I was being replaced. I thought I was losing my mind. The voices were chasing me day and night. I didn't sleep well so I started taking pills to help me. I didn't eat well if I ate at all. I smoked cigarettes like a freight train. I was a nervous wreck all the time and my hands constantly shook. I was trying to work my way into my husband love. It hadn't worked before and I don't know why I thought it would work now but I had to keep trying. I had other friends all around me that were asking if I was okay and I would casually lie and say, "Of course... everything is fine! Great! Never better!" I would spin a tale that would assure them and make them stop asking [You'll remember my friend Rebecca - she would make an appearance, in my conversations, in an effort to distract from me]. Most believed the stories or at least told me they did. I had two friends that didn't believe what I was saying. One of the two started interceding for me to God.

One day, Deceiver was getting ready to go out and ride his motorcycle. I knew that he was going out to see her. I asked him, actually begged him, not to go see her. The smile on his face was demonic [and I don't use that term often or take it lightly]. He told me that he loved seeing me jealous of another woman. He stared longer than normal - he was enjoying it. Feeding off it. He loved seeing me beg. He gained weight off my words... eating them like a meal. I can only imagine the power he must have felt in those moments. I felt I had none. I felt bound, hopeless and unlovable. I was taught this well, for years, by a very sick mind. I couldn't understand what I had done to deserve any of it. He left and was gone for several hours. Strangely I was grateful for the peace and quiet. When he got home, he told me how they were doing. His preferred insult to injury... taunting - just the Deceiver's way of letting me know that I had lost again, and he was never going to be told what to do.

I was so angry with God for giving the Traitor to me as a friend. I know it wasn't God that did this but at the time I was so distraught over it and God was the only one I could safely blame. I believed the Traitor. I felt she was like a sister to me. I felt so betrayed. The experience jaded me, made me never want anything to do with a woman again.

> I could trust no one. If I could trust no one then no one would ever get close again.

In spite of all my efforts to transform into Deedee and despite all my noted shortcomings, by my husband, he was still willing to use me if it suited his purposes. We went to buy a car and I was dressed like Deedee, hair and make-up... the whole costume. We went into the dealership and were able to negotiate a better deal because the car salesman was checking me out. During the test drive Deceiver commented that is was fine with him as long as he was able to get the car for a better price. I was proud that I had made him happy. I felt that was one for the win column. That's just how unhealthy and conditioned I was. How warped my sense of self had gotten.

My children were responding to the chaos around them. They were preteen and teenagers at this point and were already dealing with the difficulties that those ages bring. The instability at home caused additional problems for them. They knew I had no real power when it came to them. Their father had the final word. I did the best I could to protect them from the chaos that was swirling around them and prayed to God that He would continue to protect them. I worked tirelessly to keep them in the dark about what was really going on but, in the end, the only one I was fooling was myself.

An affair, cheating, adultery all so devastating and destructive to a marriage, a family. The sheer brutality and demand of this selfish act hurts and demoralizes on so many levels. Love, trust, self-esteem, commitment - all destroyed. A future now burdened with deception and more pain. I could have survived an affair, managed the Deceiver cheating on me once. My priority was that the family be preserved. I'd already allowed so much; I believe I would have rationalized that away too, forgiven him again. If only it had been just about the sex and over quickly. But it was never about that for him. I would've been willing to work through it, had my husband just come and apologized to me. But that was never going to happen. I knew it was impossible for a singular reason; it didn't serve his interests. His was a much more cruel game of power and emotional theft; it was a much sweeter victory of control to prolong the suffering of the fly caught in his web. He oozed with gloat. Who, in their right mind, would want to hurt the one they promised to love and cherish, like this? No shame, no guilt, no conscience.

The pressure was mounting again, and I was being pushed by the demands of the Deceiver. I was failing at work with him, and I was failing at home with him. I was just failing. I felt I had nowhere to go and no one left to turn to.

Things were spinning out of control.

There was never enough, I was never enough, and I was beginning to realize that there never would be. The lure of the voices in my head was getting stronger. "Quit...just quit", they would say. "It would be so easy, everything is in place," the voices would remind me. "You don't have anything to worry about, she'll take care of him... she'll take care of your children... you can go, and no one would miss you. You knew this day would come, what are you waiting for?"

I couldn't think of a single reason.

CHAPTER 7

A Clear View From the Bottom

(THE MAN I CALLED MY HUSBAND)

There are three kinds of lies - all just as destructive as the other. The one we want to believe, the one we tell ourselves, and the one we live with. In this marriage I found myself hostage to all three. There is a key that fits all three - the truth. It will set you free.

I started each day with a handful of pills, mainly ephedra... and a few vitamins. There's a joke in that sentence - I'm sure. I'd normally use humor or sarcasm right about now to soften the shame or deflect the sheer horror of past moments like this but there's nothing about self-medicating or depression I find funny or take lightly. Maybe you've been there, or have been impacted by it in some way? If so, then you know exactly how debilitating and horrible it is. This was, and remains to this day, the darkest period of my life. So many suffer silently... ghosting through life. Feeling ashamed, hopeless, feeling weak and desperate with seemingly no answer, no remedy to the affliction. As I write this truth, the past feelings of shame [even fear] want to creep back in and override my thoughts of over-coming. But no... it can't have me anymore. We can overcome, I did, and nothing will change that. I know I'm forgiven and redeemed by my Lord Jesus... the road to forgiving myself was a bit longer. My past or the pain that drove me to near madness and my end does not define me any longer. Instead, it's this tragic truth that actually set the wheels in motion for change. I don't recommend it as a battle plan but it was the bottom that gave me the foundation to kick off from. Life is strange - we never know where we'll find our strength. But it's there; we just have to keep looking. It's there; hidden by the hopelessness and despair that feels so overwhelming. I know, crazy... but true. The decisions I made after, the battle back, that's who God meant for me to be. My Daughters and I deserved a better life. I didn't know which way was up - I was so turned around at this point. I had to hit bottom to acclimate, to right myself, to determine which way was (not up) out.

So, like I was saying, I started my day with pills and vitamins, and I'd wash it all down with a diet Mt. Dew. I would top it all off with a cigarette to get going in the morning. Twenty minutes later my stomach was roiling and I knew I was alive. I almost welcomed the nausea. Thankfully I had a strong will. Sounds kind of counter intuitive to what I just wrote. It kinda is... it's complicated.

There was so much of my life I was trying to numb... the nausea meant I could still feel.

I wouldn't take any of the pain pills until after my husband left for the day. I didn't drive while using. I would pop one or two, and wait for them to kick in. More nausea but the relief was worth it.

Was I depressed? Yes, I was absolutely depressed and had no idea what to do about it. I vacillated between hopelessness and impotent anger. I was stuck. The bottom line for me was I just didn't want to feel the bad feelings anymore. The pain pills helped with that - well, at least that's what I told myself. It fixed nothing... what they (the pills) did do was sedate the moment just enough to stop me from caring about making a real change, to not care that I was dying.

I've tried to recall when I first started with the pain pills and I can't really remember. What I do remember is that I got them from all kinds of places. I made up stories to get them from people I knew, I took them from other family members and I ordered them off the Internet. I never went to a doctor for pain pills. I went to doctors for other things like anti-depressants, anti-anxiety medications and sleeping pills. I knew exactly what story to tell, just enough not to alarm them but would get them to write the prescription for me. I went to two or three doctors around the area to get what I needed. I went to different pharmacies to get the prescriptions filled. I took pills to wake up and I took pills to go to sleep. I took pain pills to kill the pain of my marriage, the abuse, the infidelity. I took pain medication to deaden the heartache of personal failure. I think you get the point.

The pressure was mounting and anything that "my friend" the Traitor thought was worth reporting to my husband got reported. He, in turn, would confront me - scream, yell, belittle and make demands that I was never able to meet. He wore on me mentally with the demands - knowing I wanted his approval, his validation... they were crushing me. The balls I had been juggling were now starting to fall one by one. I was bound by fear. I knew he could hurt me and would if given a reason. In retrospect, he never needed a reason he took a sick pleasure in doing it.

So let's rip the bandage off!

The first time I tried to take my own life, was over a bounced check. At this stage, it didn't take much to set the attempted end in motion. Yes, such a small thing but for me it was insurmountable. That's what depression does; it depletes your ability to cope. It makes the manageable things suddenly seem larger than life, impossible. I pulled into the driveway at work and he was waiting. He charged out raging. I couldn't do it. I got back into my car. He was trying to pull me out. I fumbled the keys but got the car started. The screaming and threatening pierced through me. I backed out of the driveway, turned off my phone and started driving. I didn't know where I was going. I didn't care. It's hard to explain - I felt completely separated from everything. First, I headed toward the coast; realizing that I would run out of road at the ocean, I turned around and headed west. I was going to run away. Start over. This was the conversation I had with myself. "Go west, young woman, go west" I spoke aloud to myself...for a second it made me smile. The further I got from home I started to formulate another plan. I was going to the casino in the mountains and I was going to win a bunch of money, take it back to him and then, then everything was going to be alright. I think to myself now - why did I ever think that would work?

I made it to the mountains. I had no cash to go gambling with and I couldn't go get any cash out of an ATM because then he would know where I was. I definitely didn't want him to know where I was. For that reason, I didn't use my debit card either. Instinctively I knew he would try to track me. I turned on my phone and listened to countless messages, various states of rage and then one cool calm voicemail messages from him. The traitor called too, I don't know what she was trying to accomplish other than to further my husband's agenda. It was her fault for running to him over the check I bounced instead of coming to me. Why was it any of her business? She wanted to please him too. The message that broke my heart was from my oldest daughter begging me to come home. I could hear him in the background coaching her on what to say. He didn't care who he had to use. I was incredibly angry with him for using her like that. I took my engagement ring to the pawnshop and got seventy-five dollars for it. I was stunned by how little money I got for the ring but it seemed about right, the marriage it represented wasn't worth much either. I took part of the money and went to buy a hose because I thought if things didn't go right at the casino then it was going to be game over for me; I was going to check out. Plan "A" win a bunch of money, plan "B" take my own life.

I hung out and waited for dark. I walked confidently into that casino thinking that I was going to win. The smoke in the air hung like a cloak. My mind was just as clouded. I walked around the casino asking God which slot machine I should start with. When I thought I heard an answer, I sat down at a machine. These were not like the machines I had played in Las Vegas, they were electronic and my brain, already scattered, couldn't seem to grasp how these new machines worked. Needless to say… the house won and I lost. I was so sure that God was going to come through for me; surely He understood how important this was? I left the casino understanding that it was now time for plan "B". Since it was a dry county (they sold no alcohol), I had to drive over to the next county to pick up some wine with what little money I had left. I was going to have to be drunk to go through with this. But I was determined.

I drove up onto the parkway where there were no lights. The mist and fog of night had settled in and I could barely see ten feet in front of me. It was perfect for what I was planning to do. The road was deserted. It was beautiful during the day when you could drive along and look over the valley but at night the road was windy and a little scary. I pulled off the side of the road, got out of my car, rigged up the hose through the back window, got into the back seat, drank the bottle of wine and laid down to go to sleep forever. I did this like I was planning a meal or finishing any other number of menial tasks. How bad off and emotionally spent do you have to be to feel a sense of accomplishment for completing a task like this?

My thoughts were tormenting me. Those voices in my head were mocking me. Telling me how pathetic I was, how no one was really going to miss me. See ya later stupid voices! Then, my children's faces appeared in my mind. I wondered how they were going to be once I was gone. Any rational, healthy person would have gone home. The voices reassured me that they would be fine. I tossed and turned on that seat. The atmosphere inside my car was changing and I was starting to choke. Why is it taking so long? I thought this was going to be easy. Why can't anything just be easy?

I think I was on the edge of consciousness when I was being drug out of the side of the car. The side door opened; didn't I lock it? I was pulled out and just dropped on the ground. Out of the side of my eye, somewhere in my peripheral vision I saw a being. Yeah, I'm going to say it... I know it was an angel. As quick as he was there, he vanished. Gasping for air, coughing and then vomiting, I was on my knees in the dirt, overlooking the valley on the side of that road. I started screaming, "GOD...WHY?!?" "WHY can't I just come home? God, WHY do I have to continue to suffer? I don't understand! WHY?" I don't remember all of what I yelled at God that morning or for how long. When I was exhausted and emptied of myself, my rage, my sorrow and my tears I just sat there against the side of my car. I watched the sunrise as it rose to do its job of illuminating the valley.

I felt a moment of peace. I heard God whisper, "From here we shall rebuild."

I really did hear that. I had no idea what God meant by that and honestly I didn't have the strength to really care or even try to figure it out. I had to go home. I didn't know what to expect when I got there but having been through this night I didn't think it could be any worse.

The closer I got to home the more nervous I became - what was going to happen? Anxiety and fear... why did I have to feel this way? As I pulled into the driveway, I was greeted with relief from my children and tears of gladness that their mother was home. I didn't mean to hurt them, but I knew I had... the opposite of what I wanted for them. My guilt and shame were added to in that moment. My husband greeted me with what looked like kindness. I was surprised and confused. I just wanted to lie down, but he had questions and he wanted answers. "Where did you go? What did you do? Why didn't you call us back? "I tried my best to answer the questions. Embarrassed by what I had tried to do, I minimized the explanation. When he went to check out the car, he found the hose. He came back in and acted somewhat impressed by my determination. He halfway grinned said, "You were determined, weren't you? I quietly responded, "Yes." I said nothing else. It was such a bizarre exchange between us.

My attempted suicide impressed him.

He called his sister over to inspect me. He asked her if I needed to go see a doctor. She said, "No." Then I was allowed to rest.

I wanted him to leave me alone but he would be done when he was done. He explained to me that he had called the state police to look for me, that they told him I was an adult and they were not going to even begin looking for me for at least twenty-four hours. He wanted to shut off access to the bank accounts, the police advised against it and he ignored them. He left the gas credit card on so that I could get gas to get home but turned off the bank accounts. I hadn't needed any money so it didn't matter anyway.

That little bit of "kindness" was like water to my dehydrated heart. Maybe this is what God means, about rebuilding. Maybe this is the beginning of a turnaround for us. I had a small glimmer of hope. Yeah, if you're shouting "Hey stupid, get a clue" I agree. Within a couple of weeks, things were back to the way they were before. There was never any lasting change with him. Slowly the insults and accusations started, then his paranoia reared its ugly head again and we were right back to square one. All the "kindness" had been played out because he had gotten what he wanted and everything went back to the way it was. Life resumed with our "friend" the Traitor and the pressure, once again, started to build.

A few months later, I tried to commit suicide again. It had been a very rough few weeks and he was spinning up out of control again. He was lashing out at the children, nothing was satisfactory. Nothing. He was in overdrive. He waited until we were alone then he would start. His public persona was sunshine and roses and privately it was thistle and thorns. He would try to pick a fight and if I didn't want to fight, then on to the girls he went. Critical of the most minor flaw or detail he thought was out of place he would verbally attack them. They would scurry to their rooms because they knew out of sight, out of mind - hopefully. Day in, day out... he never let up.

He placed his usual evening phone call and then came to bed. I had to lie next to him knowing this. I had taken a handful of pain pills and was lying in bed waiting for sweet relief. He had mentioned that he forgot to lock the front door and so I volunteered to go lock it. The lights were out and that was a good thing, I could barely walk. When I got to the front door and locked it, I couldn't stand and fell down. I barely made it back to bed. I lay there fantasying about what he would be like in the morning when he woke up next to my cold dead body. I fantasized about how freaked out he would be. I hadn't said a word as I blacked out.

The next morning, as I opened my eyes, I felt overwhelming disappointment. The sun streamed in and everything seemed super bright - what a sharp contrast to the darkness of my life. It wasn't even worth the tears anymore so I got up to start yet another day.

A few weeks after the second attempt it was time for my physical and I was dreading it. The only reason I actually went was because I wanted my doctor to see how much weight I had lost. Sad but true, I was fishing for complements from anyone or anywhere I could get them. While I was in the appointment my doctor did comment on my weight loss and then followed it up with this question, "Have you or do you ever think about hurting yourself?" Thinking that nothing would happen, and almost automatically, I replied, "Yes." As much as the question surprised me, I think my answer was equally surprising to my doctor. There was absolute silence in that exam room as we stared at each other. Okay, now what? My doctor quickly excused himself and said he would be right back. As I sat there alone panic started to set in. What had I just done? What is the doctor going to do about it? What is going to happen to me? My mind immediately snapped into survival mode. I started thinking about what I was going to say to get out of that office. I didn't care if I had to lie, manipulate, I was prepared to say whatever it took to get out of that office-on my terms.

The doctor re-entered the exam room and sat down. He came clean and said, "I hadn't had any patient admit to those thoughts until today". He went on to say, "I know that I need to refer you to a psychologist but all the practices that I am aware of aren't picking up my phone calls". I rushed to explain, " I *had* in past tense thought about hurting myself but I wasn't actively thinking about it now". My doctor wasn't completely buying it, I could just tell. He made me promise that I would get some counseling and of course I immediately agreed with him. He told me that he would follow up with me within a day or two to make sure I was following through with it. I thanked him for his time and left. I had absolutely no intention of going to see a counselor or psychologist for that matter.

Over the next few days, I kept thinking about my promise. The words of my promise kept coming back to me over and over. Frustrated and angry I said out loud (to myself), "Okay God, if you want me to go see a psychologist or psychiatrist then they have got to be Christian." "There!" I thought to myself. "There's no such thing as a Christian psychiatrist. I'm going to look it up on the Internet just to prove it". To my shock and surprise there was one. One! In the entire state there was only one listed and he was just twenty minutes away from me. I think I can hear God chuckling. He had me. So I picked up the phone and made the call. I made an appointment to go see this "Christian Psychiatrist".

My first appointment was me sizing the head doctor up. I seriously had no intention of really committing to doing any of the work needed to change. My life was a disaster - beyond repair. What could mere words do to save me or impact the despair and dysfunction that had become such a daily part of life? I was stuck in my pain, helplessness, and my victimhood.

In my mind no doctor was going to fix it. I went to keep my word to God. That's it. Promise kept. Check! I had no plan on how I was going to get out of going so I just kept going; once every two or three weeks. I wasn't being honest or sincere during these appointments and was just killing time while I figured away that I could quit going to see the doc. I know the doc knew that too, he used the time to try to build trust and eventually he did. I still didn't really say a lot about my marriage but I was starting to share some of my childhood to keep us both busy.

This is where the story should get better... but I attempted suicide one more time. I was still under the care of my Christian psychiatrist, better known as Dr. Bill. I was blocking and deflecting the help. I was still playing games with pills, more doctors, more anti-depressants and anti-anxiety pills. My psychiatrist never prescribed me any pills - that's important for me to mention. He really cared.

I just couldn't take it anymore. I couldn't shake the depression. I started a grocery list of "whys" with the emphasis being on what I didn't have and clearly defining the misery I was in. God, why couldn't I just feel better? Why couldn't I have a real marriage - with love, and honor and peace? I walked into the bathroom and looked at myself in the mirror. I didn't even look like myself. I was hollow. There was very little left of me. I was so tired. I just wanted to feel better. I grabbed the antidepressants and swallowed the entire bottle. Part of me wanted to die in front of him to make him pay for that lifetime of crap. There's a saying "When you hold on to anger it's you that's drinking the poison". That's exactly what I did. I walked out of the bathroom and went into the garage to talk with my husband. I told him I couldn't handle the work anymore by myself, it was too much. I told him that everything was too much. Without much care he said that was fine and he would just get someone else. It was that easy for him to replace me. I had spent so many years and those years counted for nothing. I think he saw it as an opportunity to have less surveillance by me. As if it mattered. As the medication was kicking in I felt like I was leaving my body. He said he was going in to bed and I told him I would be in shortly. He insisted that I come inside now. My words felt like pictures leaving my mouth and I tried to get up to walk in behind him and had some difficulty. My words were slurring and trailing off and in that moment my husband said, "What did you do?" I lied and said, "Nothing." Again he said, "What did you take?" I again I said, "Nothing. Come on, I'm going to bed." He wouldn't let me. He dragged me to the living room and told me to sit still on the couch. My husband called his sister to ask her what to do. She said, "Call 911". The paramedics arrived, without lights or sirens. They came into the house and asked me if I could walk. "Of course I can walk. Watch…" They assisted me down the steps and up into the ambulance. On the way to the hospital the paramedics were asking me to drink the liquid charcoal. I thought it was chocolate milk. God you are so good. They were amazed; I drank three glasses of that stuff with no fuss. I kept asking, "Where is my husband?" When I got to the hospital, I was going in and out, but still kept asking, "Where is my husband?" I vaguely remember someone saying he was on his way but it was too late… he had abandoned me for the last time. I didn't care because I finally understood he didn't either. I know - I had said that multiple times over the years but this time it was strangely different.

I'd finally given up... and I was changed.

I remember laying back and seeing Jesus' face directly over mine. It was like looking into everything that I wanted and needed all rolled into a gentleness and fierceness in His face. His gaze was direct and sincere. Jesus asked me, "Do you want to live or die?" But the question was so much deeper than that. All the knowledge of how my children wouldn't ever understand this and how much I would miss out on if I were gone just rushed into my spirit. Of course I didn't want to leave them. All the love Jesus had for me and my children filled my heart in that moment. I just remember smiling at him with tears in my eyes and said, "Of course I want to live." Then I was back in the ER but everything had changed. I immediately started vomiting and apologizing for the mess I was making. I was alive! I was no longer in fear. There was no cloudiness or confusion. It was just gone. Thank you Jesus for coming after me, saving me and healing me. I also remember knowing that I would never try to take my own life again. I just knew it deep, deep down. I felt so light and the voices were gone. I mean completely silenced. I had been delivered.

When I saw my husband later that morning the questioning started. In the blur of his mouth moving I realized, and in my mind said, "Huh, I don't miss you". I didn't miss him; that was a first. I didn't need him to save me, accept me, validate me... I didn't need him to care at all. I just remember how clear minded I was. Was this euphoric feeling of autonomy a temporary byproduct of what I had just done? Nope!! I knew it wasn't. Yeah, my eyes had been opened to a new reality. It was - clear and strong.

My circumstances hadn't changed, but I had.

It caused the man I called my husband to pause. I remember feeling like I was being examined under a microscope, but it wasn't the doctor doing it. He wanted familiar ground - I think he knew that something was drastically different and I think it scared him. He fought for a "normal" rhythm... his control language, to put things back the way he liked them. So the self-seeking questions began; he asked me about the business (that we ran together), my cue to dance to the tune he delivered. Here, let me explain; for him, this was a productive conversation to have with me because it always ended with me feeling inadequate and saying "I'll do better". "Yes my love, yes my love, yes, I'll be better, I'll be more. I'll be whatever you mold me to be - just whatever you do, please don't stop loving me". Not this time, you ass (Ooops sorry). With no hesitation I answered plainly. No spinning the answers to make it easier for him to hear. I was done pandering for his praise. Just simple truth stated simply.

I remember the look on his face. He seemed to be confused. I wasn't acting like myself. The version of myself that he was used to was gone. There was no emotion. He tried some of the usual "games" that he played. Nothing was working. As the discussion continued he got nervous, I saw it - the uneasiness in him. It was dawning on him that his world was crumbling and so was his control. He left scrambling. He wanted to play the victim, come out on top, but he knew something had changed. He went to his family, even the hospital staff, and tried creating the narrative that I was crazy. From the outside looking in it appeared to be true. He told the doctors that maybe I was bipolar. The doctors came and went, asking their questions twisted this way and that way. My husband was sending people in to "visit me" they were questioning me too. No one actually visited for the pure intentions of seeing me. They came with an agenda. I thought they were trustworthy but it turned out they weren't. Anything that was said between us, and any family member, was reported back to my husband and used to gain the upper hand. My calm nature and clear thinking was freaking them all out a bit [and me too]. They kept insisting that my stay at the hospital be extended. After a few days my psychiatrist spoke with me. He told me that he wanted me to go to the psychiatric floor of the hospital - he asked me to trust him. It was really easy to trust him and so off I went to the locked psychiatric floor, in the hospital. I knew everything was going to be okay. I didn't know how but I knew it would.

I also made a "deal" with my husband that I would stay in until we both agreed that it was ok to leave. I stayed there for the next two weeks. The hospital psychiatrist came to me a few days after I had been there and told me I was free to go. He could see no evidence of mental instabilities or a desire from me to commit suicide. I told the hospital psychiatrist that I was going to stay and keep the agreement with my husband.

In return my husband was working night and day, utilizing this time, to shut me out of our life - to take complete control and was petitioning to have me committed. He ransacked our home and the office, printed out every private journal entry I had made on the computer and had collected every notebook or journal I had written in. He brought all the "evidence" in and dumped it out in front of the hospital psychiatrist. He tried to make his point that I was insane. "Just look at this nonsense!" he said to the doctor. "These letters and numbers are gibberish. The sentences don't even make sense!" The doctor while listening to him was looking at me. I just sat there quietly, hands folded, face red. I was embarrassed that my personal thoughts were on display. I sat there watching while the man I called my husband (the one I wanted so badly to love me, validate me, and accept me all these years) was showing his lack of education and upbringing in front of this doctor... he was an embarrassment. Wow. I'd never felt quite like this before. Studying me for a response, he asked, "May I look at what you've written?" I looked at him squarely and said, "Sure...it doesn't really matter at this point because I'm sure they've been passed around to his family and read by anyone interested." The doctor picked up a notebook and asked, "What does this mean up in the corner?" I told him, "It's a code I use to keep track of the bible study or self- help book title, page and question. If you find the book, you could go to the page and question and then the answer would make sense. I did it that way so that I wouldn't mess up the books and could give them to someone else if they needed them." The doctor set the book down, asked my husband to pack it all up and take it with him. The doctor had seen enough. Furious, my husband threw all the items back into the box and stormed out. The doctor asked me, "How does all this make you feel?" I said, "Violated. It makes me feel like I've been robbed. I can tell you one thing though... it will never happen again." The doctor went on to say, "It's been my experience that there are times when the wrong person finds themselves here. I think this is one of those times." "I smiled and said, "Thank you for that." And I went back to my room.

God was good to me while I was in there. It was just God and me. It was quiet, I got to rest. God had my husband bring me my bible. He said, "It seems to me it's the only thing you'd like." I chuckled then and I chuckle now how God uses what He wills to do what He wants. Little did he know but he handed me my war manual, my play book that contained everything I needed for whatever was going on. I spent my time with God. He comforted me, He assured me, and brought me joy. He gave me peace. I'm talking about absolute peace. I felt no panic or had no racing thoughts. He gave me courage and straightened my back and legs. I would not bow to the enemy again. It was the first time in many years. I was in a locked unit at the hospital and I was fine. Praise God!

God sent my pastor, my old real best friend to visit me while I was there. I think my pastor was a bit out of her element. I mean, what do you really say to someone in this situation? She talked to me about how holiness could be found by being still and that this time was my time to be still. Fair enough. My friend came and, with as much as we had been through together, she said she was glad that she could be there for me. She sat next to me on the gurney; both of us swinging our legs like little kids and she joked with me if there were time shares available. Maybe we could both share a room next time. It felt good to laugh.

In that moment I felt like myself. I felt like I hadn't seen or heard from me for a long time. The laughter made me feel good and it was enough to sustain me.

The time came to get out. The "family" wanted to hold a meeting with the hospital staff. That morning I sat and read about David's battles and how God always went ahead to prepare the victory. I smiled, and headed for the meeting because I knew today was going to be mine. I entered the conference room and to the left of me were the hospital psychiatrist, psychologist and social worker. To the right were 3 sisters in laws, my mother in law, my old real best friend and my husband. Immediately everyone in the family started talking at once. My old real best friend and I locked eyes and an imperceptible smile passed between us as only friends can do.

My husband started by saying he felt it was important that I have someone there that wasn't his family. So I wouldn't feel ganged up on - that's why my old real best friend was there. I got to listen to how everyone was so "concerned" for me and my "well-being". The old me would have swallowed that - but history had shown that to be a lie. They wanted everyone to know that they would do anything to help me. Liars... they had years to prove that. The family had collectively decided that it would be in my best interest that I go to a state mental hospital. That was their "help". The doctor said, "On what grounds?" The family members looked like they had been slapped. My husband said, "On the grounds that she tried to commit suicide! On the grounds that she takes drugs! On the grounds she spends too much money!" The hospital psychiatrist went on to explain that in his professional assessment that there was no evidence I would harm myself again, that I had not displayed any serious psychiatric problems. The Doctor went on to say that he had told me I could leave, a week and a half ago, but because of my promise to my husband I was still there.

The doctor asked everyone to settle down. Thinking it would give them an advantage, in the Doctor's eyes, they did. He asked me to say what I wanted. It was finally my turn. I asked each one of the sister's questions about what they had seen me do. They could not answer because they hadn't seen me do anything. Another sister in law said, "I am concerned you will hurt your children." To which I asked, "Have you ever seen me do anything directly to hurt my children?" To which she replied, "Well, no." The sister he called the night I went into the hospital said, "Only crazy people try to kill themselves." My response was, "I just wanted to feel better, that's what anti-depressants do... they are supposed to make you feel better." I went on to my mother in law-the one with real power in that family. I posed the question, "If there was a way that I was under direct supervision by someone that the family trusted would you have a problem with me leaving the hospital?" She looked at me and said, "Of course not but who is going to do that?" I looked at her and said, "You. Your work at the hospital is managing volunteers. What better place for me to be? Wouldn't you agree that it would help me by helping someone else?" Left with nowhere to go she said, "Yes that would help you and yes that would make the family feel better." The staff was nodding their encouragement and agreement with the plan. I just received my first victory.

My husband, furiously rose to his feet and started screaming at his mother, "What the hell did you just agree to?" His sisters jumped up and started trying to get him to calm down. He slung the chair he had been sitting in against the wall, looked over to the hospital staff and down at me and growled, "I am done with you! I am washing my hands of you! I am not responsible for you anymore!" He stormed out of that conference room and all of his family followed trying to calm and placate him. It was a perfect snapshot of what I had been going through for years. My old real best friend smiled, rose to her feet and said, "Ready to go home?" Smiling back I replied, "Yes... do you mind giving me a ride?" The hospital staff filed by me one by one, handed me their card, and told me if I needed anything to give them a call. The social worker told me there were programs to help me out of my marriage. I thanked her for her help. The paperwork was processed and I left the hospital that day. I'd like to say I lived happily ever after but I still had work to do, far from out of the woods. It's still hard for me to believe that on the verge of turning thirty-seven I went home to a house I had no keys to, I wasn't allowed to drive and I had no access to money without supervision. I may have won this skirmish but there were a few more battles to go.

The important thing was, I was finally ready to get to work.

CHAPTER 8

Dr. Bill

(MY TORMENTOR)

I want to back up a little bit and tell you about Dr. Bill.

Dr. Bill was an amazing man. He was Ivy League educated and had both a degree is psychiatry and divinity. He traveled the world helping the unsaved and preaching the gospel of Jesus Christ. He worked in prison ministry as well as had an active practice. By the time I met him, his office was located at the back of a large storefront that was inhabited by a missions minded business. The first time I went there I thought that perhaps I was lost and really thought about leaving. Instead, I walked in the only visible door, entering the mission's office. They directed me back through the maze to Dr. Bill's office space. He was an older man who reminded me of what a grandfather should look like. I'm so happy I didn't leave. Funny how a seemingly small decision like, "I'll go through this one last door" would change my life in such a profound way.

So, I went through the door.

When I first met Dr. Bill, I was very depressed. My mind was constantly tormented - no good thoughts. I had to drag myself through the day. I pasted a smile when I thought it was appropriate to have one. I tried to pretend everything was okay. But it wasn't. I went through the motions by sheer will and guilt over my children. My children deserved so much better than this I would say to myself. Death was looking pretty good to me. That ever-present voice was right there to remind me of what a waste I was.

Have you ever felt like that? It was scary for me. My feelings were out of control and I felt powerless to change it. I felt like I couldn't muster the strength to overcome it because it took everything I had just to get through the day. I felt a lot of guilt because I thought saved people or people of faith weren't supposed to get depressed. No one in the church, I was going to, wanted to talk about it. Well, let me be fair, they might agree that depression exists and have a brief conversation but not an ongoing discussion to help people get the help they need; the help I needed. Even within the church I felt isolated. I felt that most people I came into contact with were superior to me. My husband had taught me that, and many in his family reinforced the teaching. I was listening to the enemy. I hate to admit it but when I first met Dr. Bill, the enemy was winning. As I said before, I was going to see Dr. Bill because of a promise I made to my physician and then God.

My first appointment with him lasted a little over an hour. He explained that it was very rare for him to prescribe antidepressants or medications of any kind. That was fine with me because I was getting my pills elsewhere. I lied to him when he asked if I was currently taking anything. I admitted to taking health supplements like vitamins but that was it. He explained that he generally treated people with the word of God and something called cognitive behavior therapy. He told me that he would walk with me as long as I wanted him to. He would help me get out of this depression. I didn't believe him. He was a man-just like my husband, My Tormentor; and because my husband continually hurt me I was not going to just "trust him". I thought that my counseling was going to be nothing but a waste of time so I kept the doctor at arm's distance. My past experiences with counseling as a child were fruitless and I thought that this experience would be no different. My counseling was guaranteed to fail with my attitude the way it was.

I started out with really small issues, ones that I thought would keep the doctor distracted and that way I could control what we talked about. I still wasn't totally sold on counseling and was playing at getting better. We "worked" through issues; he helped me with the stinking thinking. Dr. Bill would open up God's word and say, "Let's see what God has to say about that." I felt like a worst-case scenario for him- the really troubled one. Every now and then to begin with, I told Dr. Bill that and he would chuckle. He said, "You are not nearly as bad off as you think you are." At first I got mad at him for saying that because I really thought I was the only one in the world going through hell and how dare he minimize my pain. It also kept me from getting totally "real" with him; at least that was my justification. I wanted to stay in my victimhood.

It was still a great relief for me to go for other reasons; I would cry. I would wail. I would be angry. The sessions would relieve some of my internal pressure. Dr. Bill saw every emotion, good or bad. He was always calm. I know that he was a professional but the calm that he had was more than just being professional. He never really got upset about anything. When he would talk about the love of God he would tear up. I never met anyone like him. I've never met anyone quite like him since. It seemed to sneak up on me that I was starting to look forward to my appointments with him.

Dr. Bill explained to me that some of what I was dealing with was a generational curse. I'm sure the confusion was showing on my face. Dr. Bill explained that he had tried to help my mother-in-law with similar issues in her marriage that I was currently facing. I was so surprised. I knew the family was good at hiding things, but this was surprising because it revealed to me at what lengths they would go. Yet, I was so insistent and stubborn that things were going to be different for me. I was going to be victorious over this "generational curse". Shoot I didn't even really know what a generational curse was but I was sure ...well as sure as I could be at the time that I was going to be victorious over it. I had lasted this long, so I figured God was going to change my outcome. It took me the longest to realize that I was only in charge of me. I could not make anyone else do anything. Any success I felt like I had was always short lived when I would try to manipulate or control.

I am so very thankful that Dr. Bill came into my life. He wouldn't let me sit (for very long) in my negative mindsets. He was firm with me and would show me, in God's word, where my thinking was wrong. He gave me strategies to use to talk to my husband. Dr. Bill warned me that as I started incorporating the strategies that my husband would probably start acting out more and more.

Dr. Bill helped me come to terms with my abortion. He

helped me realize the forgiveness that had already been given to me by God. I received that forgiveness and also forgave myself. I remember feeling a dam break inside of me and I just wept. Dr. Bill gave me the space to actually mourn that death and helped me through the mourning process. He showed me that I had never given myself an opportunity to do so and how important mourning is.

He would pray over me. He would pray blessings over me. I had never experienced this before. Dr. Bill showed me what someone looks like when they genuinely care. Often I would leave in tears. They weren't sad tears. The joy that I felt bubbling up inside of me at times, it was often overwhelming. I would go back home and well, it was kind of like starting over every time I went back to see him because nothing was changing at home.

After my last suicide attempt My Tormentor wanted to go to see Dr. Bill with me. His words, "I want to get the story straight about you. I want to make sure you aren't lying to the doctor." I made the appointment and we both went. Secretly I was still holding onto hope that this was going to be the beginning of a change for both of us, and our marriage. I should have known better. You would think at this point I would have known better. I just didn't want to get divorced. I wanted my marriage to succeed.

I didn't want to be a failure.

At that appointment My Tormentor talked incessantly. The doctor barely got a word in. When he did it was to ask another question that would send my tormentor off down another trail. Every time I tried to interject or defend myself, Dr. Bill would shush me... I was so angry. This time had become my territory, my safe space and My Tormentor was trespassing. I know, I know... I had invited him. This appointment didn't go anything like what I had imagined. As My Tormentor got up to leave; Dr. Bill held me back for a moment. He told me that he would explain why he shushed me and not to worry. I was still mad about it but I trusted him and left with a certain level of peace. My Tormentor was waiting for me when I got home. He laughed at me and said, "See? Your "doctor" (with air quotes) knows all about you now and your craziness... I told you - you wouldn't get away with anything. He listened to everything I had to say and wouldn't let you say a word!" He walked off laughing with his victory. I wasn't afraid of him anymore but his words still hurt. I had to wait for a whole week to find out why my doctor had shushed me.

The following week, Dr. Bill told me to sit down and he handed me a book. It was the DSMV better known as the book of psychiatric disorder diagnosis descriptions... he marked three descriptions. The first was paranoid personality disorder, the second was narcissism and the third was borderline personality. As I sat silently and read, I felt like veils were removed from my eyes. I wondered aloud, "Why isn't My Tormentor's picture next to each description?" I remember feeling dumbfounded. I cried. I didn't think my heart could break anymore but it did. My doctor explained, "I know it's got to be a lot to take in. In my experience, any one of these diagnoses are extremely difficult to overcome but all three combined are nearly impossible to overcome." Dr. Bill would not go so far as to say that God could not do it. He went on to say, "In my lengthy practice I have only seen one person with one of these issues overcome it or at least manage it. It was a tremendous amount of work on that person's behalf; but most importantly, they wanted to get better. Right now, that is not the case with your husband. He doesn't think there is anything wrong. He has zero desire to change." It was his professional opinion that My Tormentor had all three. He went on to explain, "You will never win in this situation. You will never find the fulfillment that you are looking for in your marriage and that you will die trying either by wasting your life away or potentially caving in and giving up. You can come for counseling year after year; facing the same problems you have been facing for the last twenty years. Please listen to me." I had made up my mind. It was going to be different for me.

After I got out of the hospital I was no longer working in the business with him. I had been banned to even go into the building. I had been volunteering at the hospital and had taken a job working away from home. I started working in administration and I loved it. I was around people! It was like water to my parched being. They were not family. They were complete strangers. When I first started at work I felt out of place around people. I loved being there but just felt a little weird so I followed my programming and just worked harder to please. The difference was, the work was acknowledged and appreciated and that too was a blessing to my soul. I was happy when I was at work. I had the opportunity to forge friendships that were completely mine and I could keep them separate from home. Some of those women are still very close friends to this day and I am so grateful for their friendship. It was so nice to have women in my life that I could do "life" with without having to hide behind guarded walls. They would hear him screaming at me over the phone. My bosses were aware of what was going on. They told me at any time I decided, they would help me with the restraining orders to keep him away from work and from calling. I tried my best to hide it but cubicle walls are thin. I appreciated their concern and assured them that I had it under control. After all, it was just yelling.

There was a period of time for about six months that my husband did not live at home. There had been a huge violent episode in my home between my husband and my eldest daughter. I cannot even remember what set off the bomb. I guess it doesn't really matter because there is no excuse for what happened. He was enraged with her. He was screaming through the house and my adrenaline was off the charts trying to diffuse the situation.

Then he made a huge mistake. My Tormentor slipped up.

He grabbed my eldest daughter by the throat and slammed her against the wall. He was holding her there his face mere inches from her face, spit flying and she could not breathe. I lunged across the room and jumped on his back. Surprised, he let go of her. She grabbed keys and ran out the front door. He turned on me and started toward me with his fist drawn. I stood there defiantly not flinching - I never looked away. Looking at him, my face was cold - his face, there was just evil. I said, "Go ahead, I dare you." My back was to the wall that my daughter just escaped from. His face twisted in rage, he slammed his fist deeply into the wall. He screamed, "This is not over!" He took off out of the door, jumped into his van, spinning gravel as he took off looking for her. I still don't know what stopped him from beating the hell out of me that day. I suspect because I didn't fear him anymore, I think he knew the price would be higher this time. My defiance was palpable. Fighting someone helpless to fight back was more his M.O.

The police came to the house. She had filed a police report against him. I agreed with my daughter's account of the events. She never came home after that day. She was just barely eighteen. I was sorry that I hadn't protected her. I was proud that she was stronger than me and done what I should have done many, many years earlier. She was going to hold him accountable with the law.

The same day he moved out and into his sister's house. She came over to the house to pick up his things. I can't remember what was said between us but I do remember realizing that no matter what, their blood relationship was always going to prevail against whomever they decided.

I know that my doctor was worried about my decision to stay. Dr. Bill shifted his efforts after that "tormenter meeting" to challenge my thinking and to build me up. When I would come in with whatever new version of torment being dished out (it didn't stop while he was out of the house), Dr. Bill would point out that I didn't have to accept it. I didn't have to hand over my paycheck. I could pay the bills myself. I could go and see my eldest daughter (who had left the family home) even though the Tormentor forbade it. Dr. Bill would remind me I was a free person. He helped me find my power and take it back.

My empowerment came in small, but significant, ways.

I removed every item that my traitorous friend had given me or us. I painted some of the walls in the main living areas of the house colors that I wanted. I put my mark on them. It was my home. I made the decision to go to two churches. I went to the "family" church for my children and I went to another church for me. I opened up my own checking account and started paying bills.

He taught me the words to say to try to diffuse situations and how to walk away. Dr. Bill would make me practice saying, "I'm sorry you feel that way. Or, I'm sorry that you think that way." These were some of the phrases to use on my husband when he would try to get me to argue back. It wasn't easy to use those that terminology because I wanted to fight. I wanted justice. Dr. Bill taught me that justice would come but not by my hand but by the hand of God. My justice would come through the peace of God that I was learning how to walk in. He showed me that the real power came through self-control and not defending me or engaging with My Tormentor. It was hard - really hard. My Tormentor was masterful at the games he played. He would come and get the children that were still at home with me and take them out for dinner without me. There would be no more friends for us as a couple. He was out campaigning hard with whomever he could get to listen. My job was to stay silent. The things people would say to me. I think most of the time they were fishing for information. Eventually I just stopped talking to anyone remotely related to the situation, family related or community related because somehow, someway a version of it always made its way back to him. I wasn't interested in any of it anymore.

I kept going to those appointments. Whenever My Tormentor would make a demand of me I would talk it over with Dr. Bill. One time the demand was for me to get a drug test. My Tormentor thought I was "using" again and wanted me to prove that I wasn't. So Dr. Bill explained to me that unless the test was positive my husband would never believe the results. I asked the Dr. to order it anyway. I had the test, it came back negative and he was right, My Tormentor said I rigged the test.

One day I was summoned to the sister's house. I guess time had been served. My husband announced he was coming home. I don't know what he expected of me. He held out his hand to me which I accepted, and he wanted me to sit on his lap and lavish him with kisses. I was expected to be grateful he decided to forgive me and come home. That was it... he just came home. No apologies, no bridge building. He just came through the door like he had never left.

Six weeks later my father died. I was shaken. My Tormentor wanted to take control and tell me how I was going to go to my father's funeral. He and his sister wanted to tell me how it should all happen. They had no idea how my father was and what he wanted. I told them both, "no". I was going to do this my way because he was my father. My brother flew in from the west coast and my other brother and his family would meet us there in New England. My brother & I drove home to say goodbye to our father. I was gone for almost a week. I remember feeling disconnected from My Tormentor and my children. The only time I got to talk to them was when I called.

There was something more about that trip. I looked up and around and it was finally sinking in.

I only had this life to live and I didn't know when it would end. It was time to stop wasting it.

We had no funeral for my father. It was what he wanted. When I got back home and back to Dr. Bill, he told me that funerals were for those left behind. Not the dead. He held a funeral service right there in his office with me. He again reminded me that mourning was important. I am so glad that Dr. Bill did that for me. I loved my father and I was going to miss him. Having the funeral somehow made it okay to feel that way openly.

I kept going to see Dr. Bill but the appointments were stretching out further and further. I started, in the beginning, with once a week and was now going one or two times a month. My second daughter graduated from high school and was headed for college. Life was doing what it does - changing. I was steadily finding my independence which was creating problems at home.

Major changes were coming... and it blew my mind how fast they came.

CHAPTER 9

Abuse

(MY ABUSER)

I've had people, close to me - that know me for who I am now, say things like, "Why did you let him do that to you?" Clearly that's a good question. I mean I get it. Or they ask, "I would never let anyone abuse me." Of course, you wouldn't, not intentionally anyway. I don't take offense. I think we make these kinds of statements to help us feel safe, and empowered, to distance ourselves from it. None of us wants to think of ourselves as tolerating that sort of behavior. No healthy minded person wants to be victimized or labeled a victim. But it's a bit less simplistic than those two hypotheses may imply. So, I'll start with the obligatory... it's complicated. It's not so easy to explain, to myself or to others... much less my daughters. No one knows that better than someone currently living through it or someone who has in the past. Abuse, in any form; be it mental, emotional, sexual, or physical is scary and debilitating. Abuse is a crime against natural order, true love, and humanity. And I've questioned myself over the many years of personal contemplation, rebuilding, and self-worth seeking. But there's no better question asked then...

"Why?"

This powerful little word has led me to the depth of insight and the brink of despair. But mostly, it's helped me to realize a gradual, intentional growth about who I was, what I was, and who I am now. It's also had its counterproductive moments - making me feel vulnerable and even blaming myself... an old habit, a lie, from my past. See it's not easy - it's a process. Slow, yes, but real self-discovery that makes sense over time. To be clear, no one wakes up one morning and says, "Today I'm going to get involved in an abusive relationship". I certainly didn't. It disguised itself, "my Prince Charming", "my Escape", "my Opportunity to Have a Family", "my Chance at Happiness". What does/did yours masquerade as? It creeps up on you, grows on you, in you. In some cases, it's not so sly and subtle, in others it is. Every circumstance is different and has its own set of rules. It evolves with every inch, lie, fear, whisper, loss, altercation, touch, rationalization, hopeful moment, broken promise, leverage of pain, loud noise, "I love you", intimidation, situation, situation, and situation. You see...

An abusive relationship evolves through a series of a thousand cuts.

Imagine waking up every day to a new "cut". A paper cut, the slice of a blade, different sizes to match the pain of the day. Oh sure, at first, we have a reaction, put up a fight. That is, if you have any belief in yourself (but that's its own battle). But eventually and finally, we begin finding strength in a psychological paradox. Let me explain; "Ouch" gives way to "I can take it" or "That wasn't so bad", or "I can make this work" or (my all-time favorite), "Maybe the apology is real this time" - all justifications of an unhealthy and exhausted mind, perplexed and inundated with the harsh reality of limited recourses and a beaten down sense of self and hope. A system designed by our perpetrator to make us feel weak and trapped. We're remarkable, capable of withstanding immeasurable pain and untold moments of trepidation when given even an ounce of manufactured hope. And that is precisely where the abuser and the unhealthy mind of their prey meet in agreement. They peddle false hope and we desperately need it... in any form it presents itself.

Months turn into years - time passes and it's got you. You look in the mirror and there's the proof... you're in an abusive relationship. Denial is a powerful form of Xanax. I was too busy keeping up with appearances, not wanting to quit, rationalizing, excusing, and above all not being weak. That was my experience, maybe yours is/was different. Like I said, abuse comes in all shapes and sizes, all walks of life, all economic stature and social status. Yet we, its casualty, become secretive lepers in a system of planned ignorance and socially awkward avoidance. When do we, as a society call it an epidemic instead of viewing it as a mere social stain? I don't believe... I refuse to believe, it's communal apathy but it's something so much bigger than the elephant in the room that maybe no one knows what to do but serve coffee around it, make small talk and hope to hell it doesn't move in next door.

That said, I've had the privilege and honor to meet multiple individuals, groups, and organizations that truly care about this epidemic and are making a difference. They are heroes in my book. There are places of safety for you to go... to get the support you need. We must stop thinking of it as an isolated offense. First, you don't have to be in it alone. Isolating is the worst thing you can do, and one of the most used strategies of an abuser. Get help (see the resource section of this book for numbers you can call). Second, we all know someone who has or is suffering from this brutality. It might be someone close to you that wishes they could be honest about it - hoping someone would come to their need... even if they don't know how to ask for it yet. It's hard. We disguise the feelings of shame with a smile and makeup. Over the years I've even caught myself making light of my own abuse by saying things like, "I'd rather take a beating than _____", filling in the blank with other things like a headache, illness or some other trivial (in comparison) life inconvenience. Maybe it's my declaration of survival or what's left of my need to heal, I don't know. I've stopped doing it. I call that healing in the right direction.

My personality is one that always wants to give the benefit of doubt and think the best about people. Especially people I love. Something my Dad taught me. I didn't think it was abuse to begin with. It started with the little things:

For example, when I was a sixteen-year-old teenager I, of course, wanted to be cool. I had purchased some electric blue mascara. I put it on for my date with Prince Charming. When I got into the car, he took one look and ordered me "Take that crap off your eyes or we are not going out." I tried to counter, "It's the latest style... all my girlfriends are wearing it and blue is my favorite color and I don't want to take it off." He went on to say, (I've broken it down into "Abuse Speak")

"Well, I guess you don't really care about me..." - Manipulation

"If you did you would not have worn that because it makes you look cheap." - Demeaning

"Go take it off." - Controlling

He turned his head away from me as if disgusted by me. - Rejection

I wanted his approval, right or wrong. Beet faced I exited the car, went in and removed the mascara and returned to the car. - Leverage

Seemed simple enough it even made sense to me at the time, "He loves me that much." Yeah, I actually thought that. And I surely didn't get what I was looking for when I returned... he looked at me and said,

"That's better and now we are running late." - Blame and Shame

Interesting what stepping back, (well, many years later) and taking in a little perspective, can do for a person. That was just one simple encounter. Cut after cut, day after day - He was proficient in tactics of mental and emotional warfare. Silly that I remember thinking, "He didn't even say, "thank you" or "I appreciate you changing for me." The abuse had begun. Now, did that 10-minute moment of our very new relationship feel like abuse? Hell no! It felt like a lot of things - but most of all, maybe it felt the way I thought love should feel. What did I know as a teenager? It met some need in me, as well as, it hurting. He knew then what I would allow - it was something he could build on... I fed on the bite sized morsels, one at a time. So, we went out for the evening. I was left feeling cheap and carrying the blame for what had just transpired. He let me know he doubted my love for him which made me want to work harder to prove to him otherwise. You see? It was such an insignificant thing for him to pick on. I hadn't done anything wrong but by the time the evening was over I was left wondering why he was still willing to go out with me. He was left feeling powerful and in control. The needs of his depraved character, emotional void, and mental illness were met. We need to educate our youth. NOW!

As the days past, I made excuses for him. "He just had a bad day, that's all." "He really does care for me or he wouldn't say things like that, right?" Left with a void and no one to say otherwise, I accepted my own sixteen-year-old wisdom. I never considered what happened to be abusive. No red flag for me because I loved him, and I wanted to be with him. I considered it a difference of personal preference and nothing more. This exchange created one of the first of many dents in my self-worth as was intended by him. What I've come to realize is almost every interaction, between us, contained some small messaging about my shortcomings. Caught up in my schoolgirl love and infatuation I couldn't see it. Sad part is, if someone had pointed out what he had done wrong, it wouldn't have changed my perception about him. Being young, naive and in love is stink-bait to the warped minded. It attracts them like fish to the line.

My Abuser and I went out on a date before we were married. Dinner was great- the movie was good. We had such a good night until we went to the convenience store. There was a group of tough guys pumping gas and they were acting stupid. They were cat calling and whistling as we went into the store. It made me nervous and instinctively I knew this situation could go wrong. "Sticks and stones" I thought to myself, "They'll be gone by the time we come out." I guess he thought he needed to defend my honor and decided to shoot off his mouth. He was saying things like, "Shut up or I will make you shut up!" He did a lot of swearing too (but I'll spare you the details). I just wanted to get into the car and leave. The group started rushing toward him and my Abuser took off running. I froze. WHAT JUST HAPPENED? Panicked, I did what I do. I went into survival mode and I started talking. I got the guys to sympathize with me. "Surely you can understand guys... wouldn't you have done the same thing?" After a few minutes, I got them to laugh and joke and then got them to leave. I had won them over to protect my Abuser. As I look back it amazes me that my seventeen-year-old self already knew what to do to protect my abuser. I assured them, "No, no you don't have to hang around and wait for him. I'm sure he will come back, thanks though. "And they left. I didn't start shaking until they turned the corner and I knew for sure they were gone. Relieved, I leaned against the car grateful nothing had happened to anyone. Something ugly had been avoided. At that point my Abuser, who was hiding in the bushes, stepped out. He was waiting for them to leave and watching me the whole time!

He was furious with me. Told me to get in the car and proceeded to scream at me the rest of the ride home. "Why didn't you run too? Why didn't you go back into the store? Why didn't you get into the car?" He badgered me; he called me names, called me a whore. He accused me saying, "You want to go off with all of those guys and screw them! I know you do by the way you acted!" I managed to yell one thing back, "You left me – what was I supposed to do?" After that I could not get another word in to defend myself. The litany of blame and shame didn't stop for the entire thirty minutes it took to get home. I cried all the way back to his parents' house. I sat up all night stewing. I wanted to go home but I couldn't. I had no way out. I was stuck there until my ride came back through the state to pick me up and take me home.

He came to me, the next morning, and said he was sorry. He wanted me to see it from his perspective. He was afraid for my safety. He said he was so scared for me. He was manipulating me to accept that this whole situation had been my fault. He had done the right thing and I had done the wrong thing. No responsibility for his actions. In my mind I kept thinking, "Why did you say anything to those guys to begin with? Why did you leave me?" I was exhausted from being up all night. He kept talking and twisting things. After a bit, he wore me down. Every argument I had formed in my mind was gone. I didn't care. It was my fault. I hadn't made the right choice. What was I thinking? I'm so lucky to have him here to protect me. I am so glad that he loves me. Are we good now? Perfect. I should have taken a page out of his book and run as far away from him as possible. Oh hindsight, you are always late.

After we married, I was thrown into adulthood. I thought I knew what I was doing.

I had a lot to learn but I was doing the best I could. I was seventeen, struggling to balance the checkbook. I've followed the instructions on the back of the statement, but I am so confused. I walked up to his parents' house today and called the bank to ask for their help. They told me I did it right, but I just don't get it. Why don't the numbers match what is in my checkbook? I started to panic. He is going to be so mad. He's always mad about money. He's always yelling that I'm not going to turn out like his mother and spend everything he makes. I can only walk to the grocery store and only buy what I can carry back. How can I spend everything he makes? Will I ever make him happy? I know he works hard. Yes, I appreciate what he provides. No, I am not lazy... I am just lost and don't know what to do and can't say anything. It will confirm everything he says about me; I am stupid.

I had to wait until I turned eighteen to get my driver's license and I am so excited. I'll be able to go places now and maybe it won't be so lonely. I don't really know anybody so where will I go? I got a job, maybe that will help. But the job didn't last too long before I realized that I wanted more out of life. We made the "decision" that I would go to community college to get educated so that I could make more money. I could be somebody, because in my current state of being, he made it clear that I was nobody.

Having my license and going to school brought about new things for him to be angry about. The cross-examinations were relentless. He wants to know where I'm going, who I'm seeing, who I'm talking to, what I'm talking about. He says he has "reports" from people. What people? It's kind of scary that people may be watching me and telling him about it. Wait what am I doing wrong? I'm going to school like we agreed. Am I being paranoid? Why does anybody care so much about what I am doing? It was his constant questioning of my loyalty and motives that made me question me. I would go back and forth between, "Maybe he's right" to "No I'm not doing anything wrong." His incessant needs were both distracting and exhausting. I've also come to realize there weren't as many, or perhaps any, people giving him reports. My Abuser would make things up to scare me and to keep me thinking he had eyes everywhere.

I wonder if the neighbors in the trailer park heard us fighting. The windows are open because we have no air-conditioning. The perfectly outlined hand-shaped bruise, on the inside of my thigh, is big, ugly and hard to cover up. He got me good in the tussle and wrestle of the fight. I can't remember exactly when that particular hit (inner thigh) took place. It's such an odd place, but he's getting careless and leaving marks on me now. I find myself unable to remember all the graphic details - probably best... no one needs a blow-by-blow playbook. Abuse is abuse no matter how the bruises got there. Bruises heal, if you cover them long enough, it's the way a person is changed on the inside that lingers a while. I'm good at covering that up too. I guess I'm going to have to wear pants. It's so hot but I can't let anyone see it. It'll just cause more problems. My mom saw it though and took pictures... just in case. It looks really bad. My body hurts from the fighting. I try not to go outside too much. People stare because of the loud, degrading things he says to me. I don't want to look at anybody or have them ask me questions. I'm a little embarrassed and I don't think I could stand anyone's pity.

I feel like I'm trapped in a box.

Why do I keep fighting back? Why won't he just stop? Why did he want to marry me if I am so bad, so wrong all the time? I wish I could tell you what the fights were about. I must block it out. I can't remember all of them and I've come to the conclusion that it doesn't really matter. What matters is calm. I will agree without hesitation or at least perceived hesitation and offer no counter argument. If I do there will be a physical fight and he will always win. Remember he will always win. "Is it necessary to win the argument?" I would say to myself. Basically, he hated when I had a point that countered anything he demanded. So, he would revert to might makes right... the negative use of his power over me - using his superior strength to enforce his will or dictate his agenda without resistance from me because I was weak, and he was stronger. The truth is, my will was always stronger - it's how I survived. He hated me for that. He wanted to break me. My abuser was never interested in a marriage of love and equality - just his agenda. I was there for his needs and wants. If I played nice things went a whole lot easier on me. Just like a prison inmate.

This last fight was bad. He grabbed me in a headlock, during the fight. I tried to twist to escape; the resulting consequence is I can't move my neck. It hurts to move or turn. I can hardly lift my arms. Everything is difficult. "You must have slept on it wrong", he says. I really can't tell if he's delusional? He makes statements, like that, with such conclusion and a straight face. Does he remember I was actually there (I say that sarcastically, of course)? If there's no one willing or able to challenge an abuser, then I guess they can say whatever they want. It's now an alternate reality of truth that works for him and he simply moves on. He instructs, "Go see my chiropractor. He will fix you right up." I went to the chiropractor and dared not to say a word. The doctor asked me how I got my neck so out of whack. I told him what my Abuser told me to say. I wonder if he knows or can tell I'm lying? My Abuser was waiting for me when I exited the chiropractor's office. I was surprised. "All better?" He asked. My reply was, "It's going to take a few more days and maybe one or two more adjustments, but I'll be alright." I knew he wasn't really there to check on my wellbeing. He had to gauge if I had said anything. He liked keeping me guessing as to what he might do next. His presence was a guarantee of me not saying anything that might make people blame him or at least question him.

Shortly after, I decided, "I quit! I can't take it anymore. I'm going to see an attorney."

I'm home. Things didn't go well for me. Now I'm scared. I walked to ten different lawyers' offices in the next town over. I should have known better. His family is powerful and connected. I am nobody. They all told me the same condescending thing. "Go home. Work it out. Quit making him mad." I keep forgetting that I live in the south and I'm not an equal human being. At least that's how I feel. It's the 1980's why don't I have any power? I'm supposed to be an equal! No one is willing to help me. Sobbing, my body in pain, I'm sitting in an empty room in an empty house, I keep saying over and over, "I don't know how to help myself." I start to evaluate the situation in my mind, "I'm sitting here crying, what am I going to do? What am I going to do? I don't know what to do.

God what do I do? How do I fix this?" My heart is hurting, worse than my physically battered and tired body. When I had finally exhausted myself, I realized I was stuck.

I decided that I was going to swallow what's left of my pride, put my head down, double down and get to work on making him love me. How naïve. I can be better and do better. I can see now that was absolute foolishness. You are loved or you are not loved - that's it.

Those damn voices would chime in regularly behind every episode of fighting. "You are worthless. You deserve to be treated this way. What makes you think you deserve any happiness? Girls like you get nothing. When are you going to just accept that fact?" The enemy had me exactly where he wanted me and so did my Abuser... hard, some days, to distinguish between the two. I was silent and stuck in my head. My Abuser isolated me. When an abuser manages to keep you separate from people and relationships then the abuser maintains power over you. The abuser makes you believe that you will not survive without them. My self-worth had been chipped away until it was easy to believe him.

As a show of strength, superiority, and ultimate control my Abuser wraps his arms around me and sits down in a chair, restraining me. He won't let me move. I struggle to get away until I wear myself out - he knows I hate this. I can't move. I become compliant which just enrages me more. I feel trapped and I'm not strong enough to escape physically or mentally. It's a physical manifestation of his need for power, a game he finds fulfilling to his ego. I'm smarter than this. Why can't I figure this out?

I am a fighter... I have the right to voice my opinion. I

won't disappear without a fight. We just fought again. I called the police and they are on their way. I'd love to be able to say that I made the choice to call the police consciously. I made that call as a reaction to the fight. It was a snapping point internally for me. It was like the last vestiges of what was left of me in that moment. It was the gasping breaths of my person trying to reach out and overcome my circumstances. I felt wild with fear and vengeance. It almost felt like I was out of body for those few minutes. I ran outside the door and jumped on the hood of the truck trying to keep him here until the police arrive. In the heat of the moment, I wanted him to pay. I am bruised up pretty bad again. He still managed to get away. I went with the police officer down to the magistrates' office and filed a report. The officers found him and brought him in. He was yelling at the magistrate, a reaction of arrogance that only someone like him would feel emboldened to do. He yelled about the fight being my fault and I wouldn't leave him alone. The magistrate told him he better straighten up. They charged him. Finally, somebody stood up for me. I felt momentarily vindicated and equally afraid of what would happen next. That vindicated feeling didn't last long; he came home pleading for forgiveness, promising me it would never happen again. He disguises threats as if he's looking out for me. I would be homeless without him because he was working and paying the bills and I was not. I made the same mistake a lot of abused women do. I heard what I wanted to hear. I want normalcy - I'm so tired of fighting. I let him sweet-talk me; I let him make a bunch of empty promises of change. I eventually dropped the charges. In the eighties you were allowed to drop the charges - that's changed for the better. He got away with it again. He did what a lot of abusers do... he behaved for a little while until he thought the coast was clear.

Every time I was close to my edge my Abuser sensed it. He managed to manipulate me back to a place of complacency with shallow niceties, fake love and kindness. I want to believe it every time - this time it's a genuine change. I enjoyed the respite. The recovery period, after a fight, was always just long enough for me to start feeling better and say to myself, "I do love him". He knows just what to do to make me "happy". Why doesn't he do it more often? I enjoy when he's happy with me. I wish I could be what he needs so he'd be happy all the time. Yeah, that's the unhealthy rationalization I spoke of. It takes a while to arrive at that place but once you get to the land of delusion it's anything goes and everything is askew. I'm no psychologist but from my experience - I think our brain is capable of a great many things. Once mine decided there was no way out, it started looking for ways to adapt - make the best of it. In my mind he was still sitting on me, holding me, restraining me. I was giving in.

Now that the children are here the physical violence has lessened. He uses them to keep me compliant. I don't want my children to have to live like me. I can take it but I don't want them to have to. The physical abuse was hard on me but when it was done it was over. The mind games now are harder. They stay with me longer. I don't shake those as easily. Hell, I don't shake them at all... I just put them away. He knows I have more to lose now.

The children are sleeping just a few feet away in the trailer. We are low-voice, whisper arguing. There are times I just can't keep it in. My steam vent just lets loose. I just want him to listen. Just once. No luck there but here's a new one. He grabs a butcher knife, turns it on himself, pointing it toward his own stomach. I didn't see that coming... and he was so calm. Eerily calm. He asked me, "Why don't you just drive it right through me?" My blood start to pump and my heart was racing out of control. What just... I mean, what just happened? I'm standing there in shock. Panicked, I try to get away from him. My Abuser starts following me around with that knife pointing at him. As scared as I was for him - it did cross my mind that a man as self-consumed as he was - it's entirely impossible for that knife to go from pointing at him to pointing at me. However, at the moment, he's telling me, "You've done everything, everything else to destroy me, why not finish the job?" I thought long and hard about what I was going to say next, so I said, "What? I've done what?" I don't know I'm usually good in pressure situations. Anyway, how do I get him to stop? So, I beg him. I start begging him, begging him to put the knife away. I'm making stuff up to apologize and agreeing with whatever he says trying anything to make it all stop. He started telling me things to apologize for. This was textbook emotional blackmail. It was a very telling list of his deepest delusions and fears - thoughts of things that were not true or had ever happened. But I was apologizing for them. And just like that, it was over as quickly as it had started - like turning off a light switch fast. He put the knife away, went to bed and went right to sleep like nothing happened. I lay next to him and watched him sleep. It took me forever to calm down and wrestle with what the hell just happened before I was able to sleep. It was control and manipulation at a new level.

I never knew when or what was going to set him off or

how it was going to play out. I always felt at a distinct disadvantage. My heart would race when I heard his car pull into the driveway. I found myself constantly planning to keep him calm. I planned ways to make things go smoothly for him. I realize now that I was enabling him to continue. I would even take blame, and any subsequent consequences, for mistakes he'd make, just to keep the peace. At times I felt like I was just along for the ride. I was trading my life for a gilded cage with a hotwire running through it with a loudspeaker constantly telling me what I'm not doing right. It's psychological warfare. I've been conditioned to believe I will always lose when it comes to battling him.

When we moved into our custom-built home, I was struggling through a particularly tough bout of tendonitis in both my ankles. It hurt so bad that I could hardly walk. It caused me so much pain that it made me sick to my stomach. I would walk when I needed to in front of him and crawl on my hands and knees when he left. I was afraid to tell him how bad I hurt because I didn't want to be made fun of or accused of being fat and lazy. It didn't matter because I just couldn't keep up. He caught me sitting in the recliner with my feet up and he immediately pounced, "You're so lazy. Do you expect me to do everything? You don't even act like you appreciate this home you are getting. Get up off your lazy ass get something done..." Out the door he went. I sat and cried. The pain my body was in and the balance of mental anguish always kept me on the verge of desperation and despair.

Year after year, one foot in front of the other, time marched by. Nothing changed.

The physical abuse had settled down, but the mental abuse and mind control picked up. My Abuser wanted to know where I was at all times. He insisted that I carry a walkie-talkie type phone. If I didn't answer, I was questioned until he was satisfied that I was telling the truth. What's hard psychologically and rationally for the abused and those around the abuser to understand is the appearance or cloak of normalcy. Because what's being asked of the abused, by the controlling abuser, is often masked as reasonable. For example, while having a "work phone" seemed reasonable and normal in appearance - its use by the abuser, as a leash, was controlling and abusive. He wanted to know who I was with, what I was doing, and every detail along the way. He'd stand inches from my face, and with his angry, twisted, distorted face he would yell (like a Drill Sargent), spit flying from his mouth. It would get all over me, but I wasn't supposed to move. It's easy to stand there and take it when you retreat into the depths of your own mind. What he saw was weakness.

Sometimes when I look back, I think that, perhaps, he was intimidated by me. Crazy right? Hear me out. I was seventeen when I left home to marry him. I moved away from my home; the place that I knew to a place I did not know. He knew I was smarter than him, and that would threaten him. He exerted his control and power over me to "balance" the scales. I was a fighter. Generally speaking, I had a natural affinity for people and they seemed to naturally take to me too. He felt he had the right to tame me... like a kept animal that was his to train. My Abuser would find ways to criticize the strengths God had given me, and those he was jealous of. Whatever strength I had, that caused me to think on my own, had to go. His expectation, of me, was that no decision would be made or acted upon without his prior approval.

Early in my marriage I remember being really angry with God. I felt I had been tricked into thinking that marriage was something great that God wanted for people. I "forgot" God had said not to marry him. There was that. Many of the areas that caused problems were relatively normal issues, especially in comparison to the other abuses (at least in my mind, that's how I felt at the time). They weren't easy either, and added a level of dissention to what was already severely wrong with our marriage. There was no trust between us, and that's always hard in any relationship. He left his parents physically but not in any other way. His family always took priority, having final say over decisions a husband and wife should be making. I wouldn't go to church... I didn't like the "family church". It was small and filled with all his relatives, and extensions of the family, that lived in the area. I was always under the microscope, and ready to perform as needed. I wasn't being fed spiritually and wasn't content with being unchallenged spiritually.

I became two people, a living conflict within. The person everyone saw was happy, attentive, and cordial on the outside, but I was slowly dying on the inside. For a while, I brushed off any concerns that people had. I kept pushing down whatever I was really feeling and had everyone convinced, including myself, that all was well and good in our household. We were a couple to be envied. I lost a tremendous amount of weight in a very short period of time, as I had said before. I remember trying on clothes every couple of weeks because my clothes were literally falling off me. People were starting to think I was dying of some disease... if only I were joking. I was suffering from a mental and spiritual state of atrophy.

I tried to confide in certain people, over the years. Some even went to confront him. But he'd convince them that it was me. The ones that didn't buy into his stories would be banned from coming around. Then he'd turn the situation around on me and say, "At least you have me." I always walked away feeling like I was the crazy one. I couldn't ever really convince anyone that it was him. They wouldn't help but they felt "Bad" for me "Sorry" for me. That was never very helpful, nope not at all. I'll just say boldly, the last thing a person in an abusive and dangerously controlled relationship needs from someone is their pity. But strangely enough I kind of understood it - I wasn't able to do anything about either.

It wasn't until I broke that then it was as if part of the spell had broken too. People could start to see. Even then many still turned a blind eye - it was more responsibility then most wanted to shoulder. He had manipulated them too. I believe some were embarrassed about being fooled for so long. I've come to realize that people want to believe what they want to believe. It seems to me that even when the truth is right in front of them - people still ignore the facts. That goes for me too. There's a certain amount of commitment that goes along with caring and intervening. I get it because, like I said, I was living it and I didn't want to believe it. It's, at least in part, the reason abuse continues at an alarming rate.

God was so good to me during that time. God kept sending me people with lifelines. He brought people to me that would show me just a little bit of kindness and friendship. I kept those moments to myself. God gave me moments of rest and a cleansing breath when I turned to Him for rest. I wish I could tell you I always listened but most of the time I didn't. God's voice is quiet, and the enemy's voice is so loud sometimes. The enemy had my attention. But God saw me through it all. It's difficult, if not nearly impossible, to see clearly when you're in the middle of your storm. I can look back now and see that God was with me the whole time. I believe the people He sent along the way were like breadcrumbs to lead me out of my misery and back to God, and ultimately, into a better life.

His abusive behavior and controlling grip never stopped. It didn't matter what the circumstance was. He was never going to change. But my children were growing up and so was I. While I was in recovery with Dr. Bill, I changed - I found a better way of coping, both for my daughters and for me. I was learning not to allow the abuse in. It didn't have the same crippling affect it once had. I was purging his poison. I started seeing his attempts for what they were, the twisted ramblings of a very sick man. I didn't allow them to work (as much) as I did previously. I was still physically afraid of him but the mental and emotional games, he played, were of no consequence anymore. I was starting to rise to his challenges, and I was overcoming.

The closer to the end of our relationship the more creative I had to become. I had to hide my phone, my car keys, and my money. I had mail delivered to my work. I was closing doors and instead of building walls I was building a tunnel out. It all finally clicked, and I stopped talking. I was giving him all the information he needed to use against me for years. Well, he had no further access into my mind. My newfound self-control was probably the most frightening to him. When I was crying, hovering in a corner or pleading for his love he was at his most powerful. I had finally stopped crying, pleading or needing his love and was seeing more clearly than I had my entire marriage.

CHAPTER 10

My Father and the Prescription

(ANTAGONIST)

Playing the game of "hide my life", from the Antagonist in my home, was not easy. It has become exhausting but worth it. It's hard some days to maintain the new "me". He's waiting for it to end. Wanting me to slip up and give in. The Antagonist is challenging my new way of thinking which, between you and I, is not allowing him to know what I'm thinking. It's kind of funny in a tragic sort of way. He provokes, pokes and prods at me. It takes all my strength some days - but I won't let him back into my thoughts. He doesn't deserve that right - he's spent years using them against me to leverage more control. Do I sound crazy yet? I know how it sounds. I believe that's why so many women and men stay silent in their abuse. Better abused then nuts? He wants that. The Antagonist tells people I've lost my mind and laughs. But I know better. I'm staying strong for my daughters... they're what matters to me most. My encounter with the Lord, my God, has worn off. By that I mean the newness of what I felt, the excitement it brought, was tested against the reality of my ongoing life, which had not changed - yet. I wish I could say it was a high I never came down from... [is that even realistic?] but that's not how it worked for me. My love and belief were steadfast but there were some highs and lows to be sure. I was battling, juggling and hiding... depression was trying to creep back in. I had a flood of mixed emotions but...

> I didn't feel like a victim anymore. And that brought hope at a very dark time.

I woke up ready to put on my game face and do what I had become accustom to doing but on this particular day I received a phone call. My Father had died. I stood there. Processing. So use to being numb, not present in my own life. More processing. I remember there were bouts of time that would go by where my Father and I wouldn't talk. There was a silence that said more clearly what our words couldn't. Is that a bad thing? Am I to blame - was he? Why does that even matter now? More standing, more processing and then in my mind a voice of clarity... "My Dad is dead". I'm crushed. My Dad passed away at sixty-one, at the crux of my thirty-ninth birthday, and it was clearly one of the most devastating events in my life. We had a complicated relationship... I loved my Dad. He was never overly involved in my adult life [and especially my marriage] but prior to his passing, over the course of about 7 or 8 months, we had started talking. Not long hours on the phone stuff but you get my point. My Father and I had started having a real adult relationship. We didn't talk every day, but it's just knowing he was there, he was there... he was my "strong", a resilient man... now gone. Then, like a ton of bricks, it all hit me, all of it. I'm responsible for our absent relationship - at least the last several years of it.

I'm instantly hurting with profound grief that's trying to own its space while my rage for the Antagonist begins to build. Here's why [as I've mentioned in past chapters] my Antagonist, like so many that abuse, manipulate and control, kept our real life very private from those that only saw the performance and not behind the scenes. The easiest way to do that was to isolate me from family and friends... co-workers, anyone that could possibly help me or talk sense to me. I always gave in. I shouldn't have - but you don't know you're doing it until they own all of you, even the parts you fought to keep. My relationship with my Father was a casualty of that loss of self. I hated the Antagonist and me for that decision. I defended the Antagonist's behaviors and kept them from my Father. He knew what I was hiding, to an extent, but he didn't "interfere". That's who he was. That's who we were. In hindsight, he had no real choice in the matter... I didn't let him. But, at the time, I wanted to blame him for it. Why didn't he save me? Why didn't he stop me from making this horrible choice? I wanted to pin my marriage on him and make him responsible. What a mess... I was so angry with myself; I finally had to own my part. I helped push my Father away for years to keep the secrets of the marriage; the secrets of someone I thought loved me. I thought, "One day we'll all sit around and laugh, have a beer together. Just give it time." That obviously didn't work out. Subconsciously I think I wanted him to not only rescue me from the abusive marriage, but the abortion too. How could he have known what even those closest to us didn't know? My Father was a good man. I can see now that my Dad did the best he could do. He wasn't perfect and I'm glad. He was just the right amount of wrong.

My Dad loved me, and now he was gone.

I'm grateful that I had the months that I had with him before he died. I am happy that we had come to a place of peace with one another. I was content knowing that he was happy with his life and he was at peace when he left this earth. I'm glad I got to be part of it again. It was God's gift to me to have that peace between us. I have no regrets concerning my Father. I still... I just miss him.

I like talking about him... in this book. It's a way to keep my Dad and his memory alive and close. My Dad was not always an easy man; he was as complicated as I am. I get my sharp tongue and sense of humor from him. There were certain things I just knew about him. I knew that when he said something, he meant it. I never thought to question his word or expect him to change just because I may have needed him to. My father would often say, "I am giving you what I think you need to become who I think you are."

That seed of hope I had found was just starting to take root. I was slowly finding my own power and strength again. My Dad's death strangely made me strong over time. I couldn't really mourn with my husband; it was pointless because he didn't care. He was more concerned with finding an angle in my Father's death to manipulate and control the situation... leverage his will in my weakness. When I didn't let him control this situation, he abandoned it and went back to living his own selfish existence. He couldn't even let me mourn the way I needed to. My children didn't know my father, so they didn't miss him. That was a good and a bad thing... they were spared from the pain of loss but missed out on the love of their Grandfather. My brothers and I mourned our father.

When I got home from his funeral, I had a hard time adjusting. My grief clouded my thoughts. Depression. I know - you are never too far off, are you? I went to see my psychiatrist and yes, he helped but I was still struggling until...

There was this one particular appointment.

I walked into the doctor's office and next to where I always sat was the most beautiful journal. Immediately my mind went to, "I wonder whose journal that is. Does it have anything written in it?" My manners would never allow me to ask about it because it was none of my business. I did occasionally look at it during that appointment. My Father had been a printer my whole life, so paper meant something to me. The craftsmanship of the journal was beautiful. I really wanted to pick it up and look through it. It sort of reawakened something deeper in me, a desire to write. As my appointment was in its final fifteen or twenty minutes, I couldn't take it anymore, my curiosity had gotten the better of me. I said, "It is a beautiful journal. Did someone leave it behind?" Dr. Bill chuckled [he had a pleasant, almost cleansing chuckle] and said, "I wondered how long it would take for you to ask about it. No one left it behind. Pick it up and look at it."

I did. The smell and feel of the leather cover, smell of the paper, its pages set up with lines to write on. All your secrets could be kept here. I remember keeping my secrets on paper. It was just lovely. I smiled. Wait - to be clear - I smiled. Hadn't had one of those for a while - not a real one. Then I set it back on the table when I was done. I needed more info, "It's a really nice journal. Did you buy it, or did someone give it to you as a gift?" He said, "No, I bought it for you." I looked up with surprise. "Me? Why did you buy this for me?"

Genuine kindness from anyone shocked me, and even now it still sometimes does. His kind response was, "I want you to promise me that you'll write something in this book that's wonderful or positive or anything that you're grateful for." I'm sure that the look of discomfort was quite apparent on my face. I mean I had made a promise that I would never put anything in writing that could be used against me ever again {Remember that? I sure did]. He went on to say, "I know that this will be very hard for you at first. Tell me, what is your favorite color?" I said, "Blue any shade of blue – why?"

He said, "It may be, some days, you can only write that you are thankful because the sky is blue."

He continued, "Write in it. I will never ask to see this journal again because I trust that God in you will show you what you are thankful for. If you make this promise, I'll be able to tell whether or not you're writing in it. This is my prescription." He smiled. I tried bargaining with Dr. Bill. He wouldn't have it. He wanted my word. My word. Honestly, I didn't want to give it but once my decision was made, I quickly grabbed a pen from my purse and wrote,

"Thank you God the sky is blue." I looked at Dr. Bill, smiled and said, "I promise."

The journal itself was such an amazing gift but the real gift became what the journal contained. It continually amazes me how God can orchestrate such a perfect personal gift - understanding and loving me to know exactly how to strike deep within a damaged heart and heal it, degree by degree.

Dr. Bill was right. At first it was very hard to write in that book, and to begin with there were many entries [a few weeks straight] I wrote, "Thank you God the sky is blue". I was thankful that the sky was blue. Funny thing, I remember double-checking with the sky to make sure it was blue every day I wrote that sentence. It took time but that "book" became a beautiful journal of thoughts that opened my heart to dreams and hope. I wanted to make sure that no one would find my journal and that it stayed safe. I kept it locked in a drawer at work. Like I said, I was starting to get tired of only writing that particular sentence. I wanted to write something else. So, I looked around and randomly just picked something and wrote it down. As time passed, I was able to see more things that I was grateful for. My entries got longer and longer, I filled that journal and started another. I kept going. I began to see that things were not hopeless. My life still wasn't easy, but it also wasn't hopeless anymore. My type of depression was living a hopeless life. I think as believers we can lose track of our hope at times. Times when our life seems to be falling apart; when you're going through difficult times. I don't believe when you are a believer that you lose *all* hope. It just gets buried under all the garbage... and we get tired of digging. We forget where hope truly is; it's inside of us. When I was having a bad day, the journal became the friend that was there to show me I was still okay, and I still had hope. It was in black and white, right in front of me. The journal for me was a tangible way of finding my hope again, finding my love of God again. The writing allowed the breaking of the bonds of depression that had me so strangled at times and struggling for breath. I know now that God never left me. He was with me the whole way through. Even at the darkest. He was there that day at the physician's office, He was there in my Google search [where I found Dr. Bill], He was there speaking through Dr. Bill, He is in His Word and He is within me. He showed me the path out... through gratitude.

It's been years since all that happened.

I've not struggled with depression since that time. I'm grateful for that. I rejoice over that.

When I find myself getting a little down, I break out the prescription and start writing what I'm grateful for. Just like that, not long after, the "downs" are gone.

It took about a year to go through the whole process of my Father's estate. I hadn't really expected much to come from his will. I say this mostly because he had told all of us that there wouldn't be much if anything at all. I believed him... he was a man of his word. However, I got a phone call from my Stepmother one day while at work. She asked if I had a few minutes because she wanted to talk to me about part of the will. I said, "Okay...what's this about?" She went on to say, "Your father left something just for you. He did not leave it to your brothers." I was mildly [okay, a lot] interested. "He left you a small amount of money." I sat back in my chair and whispered, "What? Why?"

She said, "Your father told me a story that he had told all three of you, that you would have to have a plan when you turned eighteen. That there would be no more support from him financially. You were the only one that believed him. You never asked for any help, you never came to him to bail you out. And that's why he left this specifically for you." She went on to explain the particulars and that she would send me the paperwork and we hung up. I felt a little panic. Odd I know. But "What would my brother's think? What will my husband think? Will he want some of it? Will I even tell him?" were just some of the thoughts racing through my mind. It took a few days for the paperwork to show up. I completed it and sent it back. I placed a few phone calls to check on whether I had to share that money with the Antagonist and what the rules were concerning the handling of that money. I had all my mail sent to work so that's where the check went.

Upon its arrival, I opened the letter and then just sat it on my desk - staring at it. I felt protective of it. I didn't want to share. This was mine. My Father had left it for me. Not my husband. It sounds so selfish, but it really wasn't. It was the first time in my adult life that I felt like I had something that was truly, and only, mine. And my Father gave it to me. He gave it to me because he respected me as an adult... and I respected his wishes as an adult.

Dad gave it to me because he loved me.

Sure, I owned other "stuff" but to me it had never really felt like mine. It was always the Antagonist's. True or not, that's the way I felt, I was trained to think that way.

Things started changing for me - internally. Was it possible that at such a low point in my life, a bouncing off the bottom of sorts, that my Father's untimely death could somehow save me after all? Hard to think about it in those terms... I'd rather have my Father back... but that wasn't one of the choices. This wasn't something I thought about at the time but as it would turn out, the answer was yes. It took me another year to realize it. I was thirty-eight when my Father died. I turned thirty-nine two days later. The year was spent going through the estate process and gaining strength to do what was to come next.

My middle daughter went off to college that same year. My youngest, fully absorbed with her father, stayed busy - either off with her friends, tending her horse or with him. I really spent very little time with either of them. I worked, went to church, and other than that I was at home. I hid my keys daily and kept my purse and cell phone locked up in my car. I stayed quiet and small around him because conversations always ended up in a verbal bashing of insults and yelling. My nerves couldn't take it. I would just shake; my stomach would hurt but worst of all I hated me when I was around him. Accusations were always flung around. My silence toward him created massive paranoia.

I tried, for peace sake, to play along but I had nothing left in me to say to the Antagonist. I was done.

The prescription that Dr. Bill gave me strengthened me along the way. It was rungs on the ladder that I used to climb out mentally, and emotionally. Work was going well, I had been promoted and, at least while I was at work; I had a sense of accomplishment. I was happy with the work I was doing, and my employer was happy with me. It made me feel good about myself. Accomplished. I had purpose... like way back when I worked at the old smoky steakhouse

I didn't really think about it at the time but that gift from my Father was a key to freedom - a gift given in love that would one-day help open my prison door.

CHAPTER 11

The Escape

(WARDEN)

After my eldest daughter left our home at eighteen, the next year my middle daughter left for college. I found myself alone a lot. It was a mixed bag of emotions for me. I was so happy they were out living their lives, I hoped upon hope and prayed everyday that they were going to build lives that made them happy and productive. I also found myself sad they weren't around. I shouldn't have had to feel guilty for wanting my daughters to be home. Isn't that normal for most households? But who would wish this situation on anyone? My youngest daughter was fully engrossed with her horse and her high school life, as she should be. Why does it seem to be complicated? Ultimately, I was glad the two were gone because then they didn't have to live under the controlling nature of their father but, like I said, I missed them. I was getting a glimpse of what my life was going to look like in a couple of years when the youngest left the nest. I didn't like what I was seeing.

We basically lived two separate lives. The Warden did what he wanted, and everything was okay if I stayed in my lane. As long as I did what I was expected to; pay bills, keep things clean, cook the meals and above all, make no demands or ask any questions. For the most part, I was fine with that arrangement - I just didn't care anymore. Well, that's not completely true. As hard as I tried not to, I did care in short, emotional spasms [sort of like waves of breath from a drowning person trying not to go under]. But it did no good... if anything it just made me more vulnerable to - huh, I don't have a word for it... a relapse of the past - maybe? What I wanted from a marriage and family was never going to materialize. So, whatever that "word" is... that's what I didn't want to feel.

My life was compartmentalized.

Everything had its place and never crossed over into the other. I worked and had my friends at work. I really enjoyed my "work family". They would make me laugh in totally inappropriate ways about my situation. One of my girlfriends said, "GURL... you need to just put a hurtin' on him that he won't forget. Make him a chocolate Ex-Lax cake!" Oh my goodness I would laugh... it was so wrong, but it felt good. I inherited my dark sense of humor from my father and it was nice to let it out for a run every now and again. There was no way I would ever make a cake like that but it sure was fun to think about it. When we weren't thinking up new baked goods with a system-cleansing bonus, my friends would pick on me for smoking. I loved to drive and smoke excessively. They liked me regardless. Their friendship meant that I was likeable. I was worth getting to know and could be accepted for exactly who I was in that moment. In its own way, it supported who I would become in the future.

I had my church and friends at that church [not to be confused with the Warden's church that his family attended]. I was part of a large choir and the women that sat around me became close friends. They were there when I got baptized. They were there when I was hurting. They prayed. They would tease me too. Well, we would tease each other. They would say things like, "God can fix it. If He doesn't fix it then he will fix you." Sage advice. They were like Aunts to me and I love them dearly. I cannot begin to thank them for their support at a time when I really needed the prayers and the hugs. They, like my work friends, were the fuel that kept me going. They were what gave me a peek at what could be.

I had distanced myself from most of the Warden's family. I didn't allow my other compartments to comingle. It felt safer to me. It would be harder for any one group to potentially cause problems for me in any other group. I was careful to make sure it stayed that way. Yes, my insecurities were that intense. I didn't want to risk trusting any one person or group of people too much. I spoke very little at home because I wasn't going to give my husband anymore fuel or ammunition to fight over. I had run out of things to say. Why bother? It didn't matter in the end. It would always be the Warden's way. I refer to him as the Warden for the obvious reason, that's the way it is in prison. And whenever I came home, it was like returning to jail from furlough. Our interactions were hardly more than a necessity of information about what bills I needed to pay, where our daughter was going [the youngest one still living at home], stuff like that, and that was it. I really didn't have a say in what our daughter was allowed to do. He often overrode any decision I made, a power play with our child that I refused to engage in as long as she was safe. I had quit asking where he was going, what he was doing and who he was with. At this point part of me didn't care anymore and part of me wanted my marriage to work out. I still believed that a miracle could happen but even I was finding it hard to buy into that. I used to wonder what would happen if I stayed until all the children were grown and gone... then what? The image was becoming clearer. It was a cold, silent, loveless marriage and home life.

I was angry with myself for allowing my life to go this way. I was angry that I hadn't stood up for myself. I was angry that I had forfeited so much of my life in a loveless relationship of fear, abuse, manipulation and heartache. I would sit and let my mind drift, "I wonder how many of us there are in the world? Those just like me."

I remember thinking for a long time I was the only one.

What a lie! An unrealistic and irrational fear formed over years, through a process of perpetual intimidation and isolation. It's a psychological trap... and I was freeing myself while the Warden wasn't looking. I was detoxing mentally and emotionally, and I was wising up. I couldn't see yet how it was ever going to change. It may be hard for anyone to believe that I still wanted my marriage to succeed. That sounds crazy I know. I knew what God had already done in me, through my healing, and that He was completely able to change the outcome of our marriage. God is in the business of miracles. Maybe it was greedy of me to hope for one in my marriage after the miracle of my healing, but I wanted it anyway. Maybe

I still wanted to be a little pious about it, I mean what a great testimony it would make... "God saved my marriage like this..." It's so hard to explain that I could feel both ways. Internal conflict. Perhaps I was still just fooling myself. All I can say now is it's funny what the mind is capable of doing to create hope in a situation that's hopeless. So much life had been invested. I think it speaks volumes about holding on to a dream I once had, a promise I made. Why can't my dreams come true - it does for others? Thoughts of leaving my marriage represented failure or breaking my word to my twelve-year-old self. I had broken so many promises to myself over the years, but this seemed like such a big hurdle for me within. It created a line between what I wanted and what things had actually become. The Warden did not love me. That was hard for me to accept. The line had been drawn internally - permanently. In my mind's eye I stared at that line so many days - but was I ready to cross it? I still spent a lot of time stuck in my head... yeah.

One day at work, I was talking with Rosy. She and I were cube neighbors. Rosy was quiet, reserved, and had a deep sense of humor that many didn't get to see. She was a hard worker, and I was proud to call her a dear friend.

It's funny how a simple conversation can change everything.

Rosy had been through a particularly hard marriage and divorce and often she would just listen and encourage me. When two people share the same misery or similar histories it gives way to some really funny discussions and I always left those conversations bolstered and blessed. She never condemned or criticized any of my ramblings or tears... or hope. She told me, "You aren't married to a man; you're married to a boy. Real men don't act like that. Too many boys running around thinking they're men. They need to go home to get some more home training. What is wrong with these "men"? Ain't nothing wrong with you that a good man can't help... you just gotta get rid of the one you got and find you a real one." I would often blush when she would talk like that. "Could what she said be true?" I would contemplate on my own. Rosy told me her story about when her marriage ended that there were some apartments that weren't too far from work that she thought about moving to. She had looked into them herself but in the end managed to keep the home that she had lived in while she was married. She thought that I might like them and suggested I go check them out. She didn't push, she didn't tell me to do it. She offered a potential solution and left it up to me. I said, "Thanks Rosy. I need to get back to work."

That damn conversation with Rosy would not leave me alone. It came up in my thoughts often. It was so loud and very, very... "No." It caused me a little anxiety. I felt just thinking about it was wrong. Living an oppressed life had done its job. I actually felt like I was cheating on my husband for just entertaining the idea. The chains of my prison were long and strong. Time passed, I had gone through the holidays and was getting ready to cross into another new year. I thought to myself, "What harm can it do to just go look. I mean I am not actually doing it... I'm not really doing anything wrong... right?"

I laugh at myself now because it was utterly ridiculous that I had to justify this to myself.

I looked up the apartments on the Internet - they looked nice.

One day at lunch I snuck out to go look at the apartments. I say, "snuck out" because I never knew where my husband might "spot me". I still fell prey to the oppressive programming I had received. I won't go so far as to say that he was stalking me, which would indicate that he might actually have cared. What I will say is that he would leverage or capitalize on the information if he had it. Looking back, I can see that I had already left the marriage but wasn't completely conscious of it. I was using the marriage for financial reasons: a tax advantage, economy of co-living, the familiar rather than the unknown. I didn't want to tip my hand about what I was thinking, so I stayed quiet.

I walked into the office at the apartment complex and I was nervous and sweaty. I had never done this before. The property Manager was very kind. She showed me the one-bedroom apartment - it had a fireplace! It made me so happy. I love a fireplace. Little things like this may seem silly, I know, but it was like a sign from God for me. He understood what I liked and what would speak to me and touch my heart. Yes, all that over a fireplace. I could afford the rent... and the best part was they were running a special. The first month's rent was free. I could take a whole month to move into the apartment. I asked the property Manager how hard it was to be approved to rent and she said I should have no problem. I asked her if the process was private. I wanted to be assured that no information would be shared with anyone about the process. I think she understood. This kind woman took the time to explain that I would be in a safe place. She told me the only person who would know anything about what I was doing would be me, or anyone I chose to tell. Still not completely convinced I took the application back to work with me. It sat on my desk calling my name. I took a chance and applied. I faxed it back to the manager. I called to make sure she received it and she said, "I will call you at work when it comes back." I thanked her and got back to work. And then I went home... but it wasn't the same.

The call came in a couple of days later. I had been approved.

I had a decision to make. I had a limited time to act on signing the lease to get the special free month's rent. I decided to take a day or two to think one more time about it. I went home that day and walked through my house, the house that my girls grew up in. I walked through all the rooms, reminiscing, contemplating the future. I felt sad. I realized that this house wasn't a home. For me, people, and relationships make it a home. That was close to its end. It was just my youngest daughter left. My heart hurt for her and me because I knew what my decision would be. At the beginning of the next week I went to sign the lease.

I had finally made the decision to leave.

I had no idea what to do next, how to do any of it. I prayed. I had thirty days to get it done because I could not afford to pay two months of expenses for two places. It never occurred to me to just stop paying. I had an appointment with Dr. Bill a couple of days later. I walked in, sat down and said, "I have something to tell you." Dr. Bill asked could we open the session in prayer before we started. I blurted it out like it would somehow change my decision if I didn't, "I am leaving and signed a lease on an apartment." Dr. Bill sat back into his chair and started to tear up and starting to praise and pray, "Thank you God, you are worthy Jesus, thank you for hearing my prayers and answering them. Thank you for your holiness... righteousness," and he continued until he was done. I cried too. When he was finished, we both said, "Amen." He shared with me how happy this news was for him as my doctor. That he had been praying since the first day we met that I would leave. I asked him, "Why? I thought as a Christian you would've want our marriage to survive and thrive."

He went on to say that because of his experience in general and his experience specifically with my situation and family history that he knew it would be best for me. He said, "Of course I would have preferred the marriage be what God ordained it to be, but that's not always possible here in a fallen world. God's grace is sufficient for you, and your situation. You have repented for not listening to the direction of the Holy Spirit. While I believe like you that God can do whatever he wants as in doing a miracle in restoring your marriage He doesn't expect you to live in oppression or bondage either." He asked me, "Have you told your husband yet?" "No" I replied. "I don't really know how; I mean I know how but I'm very nervous and wonder how it's all going to work out. I am a little scared. But hey! At least if he throws me out, I have a place to go, right?" I told Dr. Bill that I had a month of free rent and I wanted to take advantage of that and move things that I was capable of moving on my own. I thought to maybe ask a friend of mine to come and help move the lion's share of whatever was left. I had to do this all in one day before the end of the month. He asked, "When are you planning on telling him?" "When I think I have to, I feel kind of like a coward, but I want the least amount of hell before I'm gone. What can he do? He can't stop me." Inside though I was thinking, "Could he stop me?" We finished our appointment and scheduled our next one a couple of weeks out. Dr. Bill wanted to make sure I transitioned okay and would deal with any residual fallout that may occur. I agreed.

I was often home alone, for a couple of hours, before my husband or daughter came home. So, I took advantage of that by packing things into the trunk of my car. The trunk was not visible so I could take things out in secret. I would then take my lunch and deliver them to my apartment. I did that for two weeks.

The time had come for me to tell him.

I waited until he got home, and our daughter was off in her room. I went out to the garage where we both smoked. There was no easy way through this except straight through it. I summoned up my courage, looked at him and said, "I am leaving. I am moving out. I have an apartment already and will be gone by the end of the month." I saw surprise on his face.

It was a satisfying feeling even though my insides were shaking. He said, "Really? How are you going to move out?" "I have made arrangements with my friends to come and get my things. I am not taking much." I said, as if I wasn't allowed to take anything at all. "Who is going to help you?" I told him. He nodded his head and went back to his cigarette. I knew I had been dismissed and walked back into the house. I was relieved, sad and angry all at once. I had told him it was over, and I was relieved, I was sad because it didn't seem to matter to him, and I was angry with myself for having waited so long to make this life changing decision. It's like having the keys to the cell door and believing you can't use them.

The next day when he came home, he asked me to come out to the garage. He told me, "You aren't leaving until you have a separation agreement in place and your "friends" are not going to help you move out. If, you get the separation agreement done then I will be the one to move you out." He went on to say, "You will be paying for the separation agreement." He asked me if I had told our daughter. I said, "No, I was going to talk with her and ask her who she wanted to live with." I immediately felt defiant and told him, "You cannot stop me." He said, "I will have you on abandonment and I will make sure you get nothing." In that moment I realized he had been to talk to someone. I should have known, a game of advantage and leverage, what a surprise. The conversation - my mistake - the Warden's demands for release, only sealed my resolve to leave.

I did ask my daughter. She was a young teen; she wasn't happy that her parents were getting divorced, what kid would be? Her world was going to be turned upside down. I understand because I felt the same way when my parents divorced. My daughter decided to stay with her Dad. I understood. I did not try to persuade her, I did not "fight" for her to come with me. I felt at the time it was best for everyone to leave it be. I didn't want her in the middle of a battle. I wanted her to be able, to be where she felt most stable. Did I make the right decision? I've often wondered over the years. What I do know is she was safe, and that the choice did what it was intended to do... it allowed her a level of stability that, well, it made the rest worth it.

I really don't believe he thought I would get the agreement done - but I did. I went into making that agreement with the understanding that the better I made it for him the more easily he would sign it. So, I sat and thought about what I really wanted. I wanted to know that my children would be cared for in their education. I didn't want to pay child support. I was leaving the lion's share of assets uncontested with him. I wanted my car, my personal effects, and half of the proceeds of the sale of the family home. Some of my friends told me I was making it too easy on him, that I had a right to more. He could have everything else. I figured if the Lord wanted me to have those things, I was leaving behind then He would be the one to see that those things would be restored to my life. I felt like I had paid a high price with my life and the "stuff" wasn't worth it. I knew he'd think I was stupid but that's what I wanted him to think.

We went to the attorney's office. I had explained, previous to the appointment, what was most important and what he could have; which was basically all of it. He thought he deserved everything. He demanded everything. And while it may look like I gave him everything he wanted, what I wanted was a fight free exit... I was weighing "stuff" against a war. And I believe a battle is what he truly wanted. I knew what I was giving up. I did not want my daughters to suffer any more than what the divorce would cause to begin with. I just wanted peace. So, I did what I had to, I gave him all the stuff. The thought of it being the last time I'd have to do it was enough for me. Some may say I acted out of fear. Yes, I was afraid. There is no shame in fear. I kept my courage, and my eye on the ball. I knew what I wanted.

The agreement was signed, I was moving out.

I remember having one last conversation with him about us. It took place in the garage just like so many others had - we joked. We joked about what if over the next year we were able to work it out? Wouldn't everyone be surprised? It was kind of a pathetic conversation as I look back. It was a game just like all the other games. Lull me into a sense of complacency and then leverage the situation to get what he wants. Have you ever had a moment that you went along with the conversation even though deep down you knew it was a lie? It was that type of conversation. I was just serving him back a slice of the pie he had been feeding me for too long. He certainly knew my weaknesses and was still willing to use them to his advantage. In his mind it made him feel superior. I must be honest though... there was still a sliver, the slightest glimmer that maybe, just maybe, it could come true. In the recesses of my mind I thought, "My show of strength could fix things. He wasn't expecting it and my absence would show him."

The day I moved in, right before he left for the last time, he dropped off a pile of bills. He said, "You were still living in the house generating these bills, so you didn't think you'd get by not paying them did you?" "Of course not, because the bills and money are always more important than the relationship, right?" With that he walked out the door closing it behind him for good, and for once not saying a word.

I was one month away from turning forty.

Those first few nights in my new apartment I just sat on the sofa. In the quiet, no demands, no asking, no nothing. I just sat there. It was the first time I just felt exhausted and exhilarated at the same time. The atmosphere was ripe with "what do you want to do?" At first, I had absolutely no idea. I went to work. I went home. I went to church. I went home. I sat in silence. I enjoyed it. My work friends and church friends were a little worried about me. Why was I spending so much time alone? Because it felt good and...

I was free.

This is silly but I ate what I wanted, when I wanted and didn't if I didn't want to. I set everything up the way I wanted it. I didn't have to ask, negotiate, or receive rejection over any decision I made. It was what I wanted. It made me feel giddy. I left things out on purpose, out of place just because I could and there was no one to say a word. Nothing had to be "perfect" anymore.

I could take a deep breath and figure out who I was. I

mean, I kind of knew who I was but reintroducing myself to me was important. I didn't really have an idea of what direction I wanted to take my life. I felt like I had so many choices right there before me... I had choices to make for my life.

I missed my youngest daughter and called her every day. I talked to my other daughters daily. I was living the honeymoon of my new life.

I was happy.

CHAPTER 12

Year One

(SORE LOSER)

The major life milestone of turning 40 is often a time of reflection and transition.

I turned forty less than a month after moving into my very own apartment. There was a lot of transitioning but not a lot of reflecting going on - not yet. I was too busy being introduced to someone I had an estranged relationship with for many years... me. Some might find the big 4-0 to be a sad, or even depressing, birthday to celebrate. For me it was my promised land. Let's just say, I can definitely see some similarities between the Israelites wandering the desert, longing to find home, and my previous forty years. Okay, I won't over spiritualize it, but I'm inclined to think it was a result of God's plan for my life being fulfilled. The "detour" was complete and now I was back on track... I was happy. I was building a life, something that belonged to me. But I was completely unaware I was still dealing with stuff the surface joy can't fix overnight. There needed to be balance... I didn't find that at first.

Let me back up to - "God's plan for my life being fulfilled." I never want my children to think they weren't part of God's plan. They were the best part of God's plan. That will never change. In the midst of it all - they were my hope and purpose, my joy and my strength. I love my children beyond words. I believe they know that. I'm blessed to have had them and continue to have them in my life... each in their special and profound way. I know that God blesses and redeems. God loves me so much that he redeemed a poor life choice and blessed me in ways that no human can. He blessed me with my daughters... and eventually my freedom. Free to now live a life more abundant. I didn't want my daughters to look at me and be ashamed. I felt so powerless and humiliated, for so long. I didn't want them to think it was normal to live the same life I had, allowing someone to control and abuse them. Yes, I made many mistakes - perhaps the biggest of them being too afraid to leave sooner. What if living in it everyday (as they had) could somehow make it easier for them to accept in their own lives? That thought was bone chilling and nauseating. It wasn't too late. I was ready to live the kind of life that allows me to role model for my daughters what it means to be in a loving relationship... first with yourself and then with someone else. To be an empowered, devoted woman not a pawn in someone's psychologically damaged game of control.

My birthday turned into a month of celebrating. I wore the word "Celebrate" out. My work friends took me out and we had fun. Have you ever seen a child's reaction, in a toy store, and the words "Get whatever you want" are said? I never had the "young adult" experience of going out all hours of the day and night. I did in year one. I found myself making up for lost time - not in a crazy get blackout drunk every night, promiscuous sort of way... not my style. I didn't want that. I also didn't want to say no to anything that sounded like fun. So, I didn't. We ate out and "bar hopped". I laughed really loud, so loud - I caught myself... a weird self-awareness kinda thing. As if I remembered I wasn't supposed to do that... laugh like that. So, I laughed even more. My friends told every bartender along the way that it was my birthday. I was happy and embarrassed at the fuss being made over me; make no mistake I secretly loved it. As the night went on, I lost count of the number of times that my friends sang happy birthday to me, with the help of whatever bar we were in. I'd never done that, ever. I drank this drink called "hypnotic" and collected glow sticks over the course of the evening that came from the drink. My friends drove me home, at two o'clock in the morning, where...

I fell into bed and slept until lunchtime.

Sleep. I only mention this because I've always just accepted my bad sleeping habits as normal. By that I mean I rarely had a good night's sleep. For years I struggled with sleeping through the night, it was hard. Okay, this night I had been drinking - that certainly didn't hurt, but it was more than that. I started to realize, as I felt more and more safe - safe from something nameless that seemed so much bigger than me - I was starting to rest through the night, every night. That alone was life changing.

Then I went out and celebrated with my church friends. They took me out to eat Greek food. I had never had Greek food - I loved it. I got birthday presents! I still have one of those presents to this day. It's a colorful, cheery mug that reminds me to be cheerful and quirky too. When I went to choir practice, my choir director had the entire choir sing happy birthday to me. The experience made me emotional. My choir director said, "We won't ask how old you are..." To that I responded loudly, "Forty! I am so very glad to be forty!" That whole first month was emotional and good for me. My spirit was soaking up the love and attention.

I went out with my daughter and husband too (we weren't divorced yet). It was weird celebrating with him. I wanted to go out with just my daughter but because she couldn't drive "it just made sense" for us to all meet at the restaurant. I hate to admit this, but I didn't even think about it being his way to control the interaction or troll for information. When would I learn that he was always looking for leverage? I know that some might think I am just being paranoid, but I knew better. I'm thankful I drove myself and was able to leave when I wanted. I may sound bratty, but I didn't want to celebrate with him, and frankly, why should I? To keep the peace, and because I wanted to celebrate with my daughter I went with no argument. He was good at leveraging any situation and I was proficient in letting it happen.

When I fully realized that I was free; I turned into a kid in a candy shop. I went places I wanted to go, did things I wanted to do. I even did silly things (that meant something more to me) like, if I didn't want to prepare dinner or eat that night, then I wouldn't. If someone invited me somewhere - Yes! I would go. I challenged, what I called my "permission" reflex. If I wanted to go to the movies, I would go. I was honestly going day and night. I didn't want to stop because I felt like I had to make up for all the lost opportunities and just went, went, went. Given the circumstances the pendulum was in full swing. Balance. Was. Needed. Queue Dr. Bill.

I was still meeting with Dr. Bill and would excitedly tell him about all my adventures both at work, outside of work, church... everything. He was my confidant and one of the wisest people I knew. He was so happy for me at first. I showed up for an appointment one day and started to regale my adventures. Dr. Bill asked me, "When was the last time you were still? Are you sleeping? Have you taken time to rest?" I told him, "I'm fine! I'm so happy, and happy to be going and doing whatever I want." Dr. Bill went on to explain that I was responding to a void. I had lived in an environment for so long that was high pressure, intense and filled to the brim with posturing for peace. It was time to learn how to live at peace. I was using my "going and doing" to cope, instead of being intentional with my life. I knew he was right; I didn't want to admit it though. Once again Dr. Bill came to my rescue.

"I want to assign you some homework." Dr. Bill said.

"Okay... what is it?" my mind already made up I wasn't going to do it.

"I want you to sit home all weekend, except for church. No going out Friday night, all day Saturday or Sunday, with the exception of church. I want you to sleep in. Take your time, watch television, lay on the couch... get it? I want you to do pretty much nothing."

"What?! I can't do "nothing" ... I don't want to do nothing." I whined.

"Don't you have a fireplace?" He asked.

"Yes. Why does that matter?"

"Get a bundle of wood, light a fire and enjoy it. I want you to learn how to just be and relax. I know this is going to be hard for you. I know that you can do it!" He chuckled - I scowled.

"Promise." He said.

Why did he always want me to promise him?

"Fine. I'll try."

"No, you'll do." He firmly stated.

"Ok, fine...geez, I'll do it." I knew it was for my own good. I was just having so much fun.

That weekend, wow, it was hard. I drug my feet at work on Friday. I actually worked late-on purpose. I stopped by the store and picked up a couple of bundles of wood, a bottle of wine and a frozen pizza, and went home. I walked through my door, and as I closed it, I said to myself and God, "You're gonna have to help me with this." [I have to laugh at myself because now I'm such a homebody]. I like being at home. I would rather have people come to my house than go to theirs... mostly. I poured myself a glass of wine, started the oven and went searching for some paper to burn. I started a small, calming fire, and sat on the floor. Then I had a brilliant idea to start burning stuff. I went through newspapers and burned them. I hadn't lived there for very long but somehow managed to build a nice stack. I was bored. After a few minutes of feeding the once small, calming flame - It got so hot in my apartment I had to keep the patio door open just to stand the heat. I never cooked the pizza that night, instead I made popcorn, had another glass of wine and waited for the fire to burn down. I closed the patio door and went to bed to sleep until I woke up the next morning.

The sun was bright, peering through the window across my bed. Stretching, I just kind of looked around, thinking, "What am I going to do today?" Then I remembered. Nothing. I was going to do nothing. I spit raspberries into the air. I groaned, "Why did I have to promise?" Rolling around on the bed like a little kid. It was like I could hear the Holy Spirit laughing at me. "HA! HA!" I yelled out loud with as much sarcasm as I could and got up. I opened the fridge, "Hmmm, what am I going to have?" I said out loud. "He didn't make me promise to keep quiet; I could talk on the phone all day, now couldn't I?" I settled on bacon, eggs, toast and a cup of tea. Sitting on the couch Indian style munching on my breakfast, I turned on the television. Click, Click, Click as I rolled through remote. "Oh my God, this is so boring... "It's going to be a long weekend and it was only eight thirty in the morning. I think God was already sick of my complaining because after I ate, I stretched out on the couch and the next thing I knew it was like one o'clock in the afternoon. I woke up dazed thinking, "What? What time is it?" It was almost a panic feeling. I felt like I shouldn't have been sleeping and was in trouble for doing it. I laid there thinking about that. I got mad at myself for being like that. "Of course, you can fall asleep. Who cares? Who am I "in trouble" with?" Then I thought about Dr. Bill, "I wonder if Dr. Bill knew I would go through this." I chuckled. "Of course, he did." I took a deep breath and reminded myself, "I am free." I was free to go; I was free to stay. I was free to rest. The rest of that Saturday I piddled around. I ate, I took another nap, I watched movies, I cried at the movies and a little just because. I finally fixed the pizza for dinner, ate, made a fire and went to bed. Surprisingly, after all the rest I had gotten, I fell into a deep sleep.

Sunday morning, my eyes popped open and I smiled. "Yay I get to go to church today!" I said to myself. "I get to get out of my apartment for a while today." I danced out the door and down the stairs to my car. That was the first time I went to both first and second service, sang in the choir both times, hung out until I was one of the last people to leave church and headed back home. It was about one-thirty in the afternoon, and I was starving. I made myself a sandwich, sat on the couch thinking about how I outsmarted my agreement with Dr. Bill. I mean he did say I could go to church. I stretched out on the couch and yep... you guessed it, out like a light! When I woke up the sun was headed down and I realized I had made it. I had kept my promise. I ate dinner, set things out for the next morning and called it a day. I couldn't wait to tell Dr. Bill all about it. God had helped me get through it. You know, come to think about it, no one called me that weekend. It was just God and me.

I know this may not seem like a big deal to some - okay, so I sat home for a weekend - but it was to me... especially now that I look back on it. A small seed grows roots. This was the beginning of a healing process. It was one of the simplest, yet deeply important moments in my walk toward something better. It's all about perspective. I had to know, believe this newfound life wasn't going to be taken away; I didn't need to live all my happiness in a year. I had to stop and breathe, take it in. After so many years - it just didn't seem possible. So, I ignored (drowned out) the voice that said "It's not going to last" by staying on the go. That little voice lied often to me over the years - it taught me to fear the unknown and to stop trusting myself. I was ready to leave that behind me too. This was my life to live, I didn't need anyone's consent to be happy... for the first time, in a long time - I was enough. I needed to grow not hide or run or ask permission from anyone but me. What I was doing would have eventually burned me out and had the potential to truly hurt me over time. Leaving one extreme into the open arms of another was not what I needed, not what I wanted. It was my first steps toward equilibrium.

At my next appointment I told Dr. Bill all about it. He laughed so hard when I told him that I had outsmarted the agreement while at church. He said, "I'm glad you told me because it's not too often that someone works as hard as you did to get around an agreement that you made, and you used "church" to do it. I just wanted you to learn that from here out you get to choose. It's okay to rest and that you can do it. God wants us to rest. It is important to rest."

I asked him about the panic I felt that first day. He explained that even though consciously I knew I was free; my mind, subconscious, and emotions were still catching up. There are layers of healing still needed. Over time my mind, my will and my emotions would come to that same understanding. The panic response I had, the first day, didn't surprise him. He asked me, "What did you do?" I went on to tell him that I had gotten mad at myself and had told myself to, "Get over it." He said calmly, "You know... it's okay to be kind to yourself. I mean considering what you've been through. Why not just try to accept that these feelings are going to rise, acknowledge them, and say to yourself, "I am just re-learning how to live" because you are. "

Honestly, that was hard for me to accept and do. Why couldn't I just do it? I just thought that when I left the marriage, I would be instantly better. I was, in some ways, but the old programming would still rear up. Even still, all these years later, there are still whispers of that programming that I work through. Dr. Bill was there to remind me that I was in unchartered territory for myself. I had never lived on my own. I had never been fully in charge of my own life. I had a lot to learn. It was exciting and scary... but that's life I suppose.

It wasn't too long before my new life honeymoon was going to be over.

As crazy as it sounds, I had still harbored some distant hope that perhaps the Sore Loser and I could work things out. It had been some months, and for the most part, my soon to be ex-husband had left me alone. I started to soften towards him. In my car, on the way to Easter choir practice, my phone rang. I looked down to see I had a voicemail. I checked and didn't see that I had missed a call. So, I called in to listen to the message. It was a conversation between my husband and either his sister or his girlfriend (they sound alike). I'm pretty sure it was the girl friend. They were talking about me, "Chris thinks she so smart, well I have news for her. She is gonna pay. She will never come back into this house. I am done with her." The woman just vehemently agreed with everything he said. That seems familiar. Where do I know that from? Oh, me. I used to do the same thing. The message lasted about four or five minutes. It was awful. The things said were hateful. I sat in my car and cried. It was the wake-up call I needed - at a time I could receive it. It was the final nail. The marriage was dead, my hope in "us" was dead, and my tears were witness to my embarrassment. How silly and naïve I was being, so hopeful for something that was long since gone. The mourning I began to feel was very real - the reality of loss was finally able to happen. I let it happen right there in my car. I didn't want to go to choir practice. So, there I sat in the parking lot, my face a mess, when my choir director knocked on the glass.

"You okay?" He said

Shaking my head "Yes", I said, "No." It was complicated. Then I forced out, "I just realized that my marriage is really over, and my husband is a hateful man."

He said, "I am so sorry to hear that."

"Yeah, me too." - it seemed the right thing to say.

"Come on inside, just sit when we sit, stand when we stand, you're where you are supposed to be. Whatever happens, it will be his loss. No one is going to say anything to you, I promise. Give me a couple of minutes and then just come in and take your seat."

I nodded my head but was unsure. While I was waiting, I tried to fix my face. The feeling I had was the same as the first day I walked into Dr. Bill's office. Not sure what to expect but sure I had nothing to lose and perhaps everything to gain. I walked in, took my seat. No one said a word, but my church friends slid their arm around me, in my chair, and gave me a squeeze. They took my hand when I stood. By the time the practice was over I was singing again. Having the proper support system around you is half the battle - I wasn't completely over it that was my half to deal with. I had come quickly to the place of acceptance. It was over and I was going to be alright.

I have to admit; even though I felt better I was so stinking mad. It was like a lid had come off a pot of simmering venom that I hadn't wanted to admit even existed. I wanted to spew it everywhere. I felt vengeful. I wanted to make him pay for every wicked thing he had ever done. Those buried feelings finally started coming to the top. I wanted to be nasty to him. My anger also kind of scared me a bit. I was so used to being on lock down with my emotions that for them to just spring free was kind of scary. I took the next few opportunities to goad and be nasty with him. I was short in our conversations and I even hung up on him a time or two... something I would have never done before.

I was talking with friends about how mad I was. They told me I really wasn't being that bad to him. They reminded me of what I was giving up to divorce him. They reminded me of some of the phone calls they overheard. It really wasn't helping me that much, if anything it just made me angrier. I don't know if you're like this or not, but if I cry when I am angry, it's bad. I was allowing anger to control me, and it didn't feel good at all. God didn't allow me to stay there too long. He had a plan.

I went to bed one night and had this amazing dream. The dream starts out with me walking along the beach holding a big white wicker laundry basket. Off in the distance I see a figure and I just kept walking. We were walking toward each other. It was such a beautiful day in my dream. The sea breeze, the warm sun, wet sand under my feet and the sound of gentle waves... anyway, we just kept walking toward each other. When I was close enough to see, I realized it was Jesus. I ran the rest of the way to Him and was so happy and excited to see Him. He turned around and continued to walk with me the way I was going. We walked silently for a few minutes - like good friends can do with one another.

He stopped and asked me, "What are you carrying in the basket?"

I looked down and realized I was still carrying that basket. I realized it was heavy. I had almost forgotten it. I looked into the basket and it was much deeper than any ordinary basket. It was filled with filthy, twisted, dark things. The items didn't really have a shape; they were just kind of twisted almost life like. I looked up and said to Jesus, "Nothing." I felt ashamed of what I was carrying. Jesus held out His hand and asked, "Would you give me just one?" There was no judgment or criticism, just love and kindness. I took a look into that basket again, unsure; I picked up one of the smaller twisted, nasty, things and slowly handed it to Him. He said, "Watch this!" He took that twisted dark thing and flung it like a Frisbee over the ocean and it burst into a spectacular firework spray. I giggled with glee; because I love fireworks, and this was the most beautiful I'd seen. He looked at me and asked, "May I have another?" I took another out of the basket and handed it over, anticipating what would happen again. Yes! It burst into fireworks. I was having such a great time.

I started taking those twisted things out of the basket faster and faster, handing them to Jesus to turn into fireworks. I just felt lighter and lighter the more He cast those things over the sea. I hadn't realized how much weight I had been carrying. The basket was finally empty. Jesus and I continued our walk down the shoreline. We were laughing with one another about what had just happened. I was swinging the empty laundry basket as we walked. Jesus stopped again and looked at me. He said, "Give me the basket." I remember looking down at the basket and saying, "What if I still need it?" He smiled that smile that only Jesus can smile; the kind that reaches down into the deepest part of me and warms me from the inside out. He said, "Trust me, you won't need it again."

He said, "Do you trust me?"

I said, "Yes." I handed him the basket and he flung it out over the waves and it too became a fireworks display but this was even more brilliant than before. I instantly woke up. It was dark in my bedroom. I was both happy and a little sad because I wanted to go back and be with Jesus on the beach. I laid there for a few minutes and realized that something had changed. I had changed. My anger was gone, and I peacefully drifted back asleep. After that dream, my anger really did go away. I still had to deal with the particulars of going through a divorce and all the skirmishes and battles that were still left to go through, but I wasn't really able to hold onto my anger past that moment. I think it's because, psychologically, I had nothing left to carry it in.

The next several months brought challenges. The Sore Loser still tried all the same tricks and schemes; mostly, they didn't work on me the way they had in the past. I can't say I was impervious to all of them because in weak moments well, you know.

He would try to make me feel bad about the good that was happening in my life. He would escalate like a small child not getting his way - the name-calling, threats, and attempts at manipulation. I knew it was over. I knew that once the divorce was final, I would have to cut him out completely, no contact with him at all. That is, if I ever wanted to truly be free of the shaming and ugliness he embodied.

Those same months brought blessings too. It was during this time that I met a man that would later become my husband and for all the efforts of the Sore Loser, I was happy. As I think back, my current husband really did love me through that time and through some messy stuff. I'm sure that wasn't always easy for him. He stood with me, and encouraged me, to be who I am. He held my hand when I needed reassurance. He cared for me. He was my sounding board and a solid foundation for me to rebuild. I was able to share my love with him without it resulting in some form of hurt, shaming, fear, pain or head-games... no pretense just love and honesty. That took some work and soul searching for me. It's hard to live most of your adult life playing in a high-stakes game, without thinking there's an angle being played somewhere. He helped me to see that some people are just plain good.

As that first year came to an end, I had much to be thankful for.

I was only a few months away from the divorce becoming final. The Sore Loser took any and every opportunity to leverage and delay the inevitable... his newest game to be played. I let him play it alone. I never understood why... was it just so hard to lose? He did the same with the sale of our home. But try as he might, both came to a conclusion within a month of each other; the house was sold, and the divorce was final.

I was completely free of him.

I took that opportunity to close the door on the relationships with all the extended family, as well as, him. It was better for me, and I was going to make sure it stayed that way. It took him a couple of years; it was difficult for him to concede his control over me. He tried all the old tricks and a few new threats but found they fell on, now, deaf ears - and nothing ever came of it. It was truly and finally over.

Author's Reflection

Can We Talk (My Past)

Prince Charming, Heartache, Man of My Dreams, Deceiver, Man I Called Husband, Tormentor, Abuser, Antagonist, Warden, and Sore Loser. I had a lot of names (descriptive titles) for my Ex but ultimately, he has become My Past, and motivation to help others. When I think back, I really wanted nothing more than to love and be loved. By the grace of God, I have that now. I'm sure you have some colorful and pain-induced adjectives of your own, to describe your battle. I decided not to use real names for three reasons:

First, I didn't want this book's account to interfere with my daughters' lives. Nothing is worth placing them in a possible situation that could hurt them or alter what they want for their lives. Speaking out is my choice... not theirs. It had to be done to fulfill a calling I've had deep inside for many years. And My Past has the right to his privacy too.

Second, I came to realize. I was not unique in my circumstance nor was I ever alone. God was with me in that season. Sadly, there are many of us living the same or similar lives of abuse, dysfunction, and psychological control. Each year, there are thousands of newly reported cases of abuse and countless untold stories inflicted on those too fearful or embarrassed to come forward. My Past, he's not significant or different; he's as common as any coward. So why treat him as if he deserves distinction? A person that hurts someone for their own demented reasons of manipulation, control, satisfaction and/or selfish gain (rather than be physically, sexually or psychologically) are the same. They're called by many names, but still all the same. They are rich and they are poor, and still the same. They have tragically become who they are for a vast variety of reasons, yet the same. They're the same because they harm and destroy; taking unsuspecting lives off the course of fulfillment. Until they acknowledge the truth, repent, get help, and stop hurting others... they are the same. I do, at some level (usually in prayer), feel for those that struggle with the desire to harm others. A vast majority are victims of abuse themselves. There's no excusing what they do. As adults, civilized human beings, we have choices to make and we all must take responsibility for them - no excuse, but it is a fact. My Past (my Ex) is the same as yours... and if I can find my blue sky, trust me, so can you. I want you to know that even when the sky is gray or there are heavy storm clouds in your life, above - there is a blue sky. There is a place to begin your journey out from where you hurt.

And third, I didn't write this book for revenge or some form of payback. Never really my style - though I did laugh pretty hard at the thought of that "ex-lax" cake. There's bigger fish to be fried and a point to be made here, and that point is awareness. I wrote about my experience to bring attention to an increasingly more common problem, a problem that's been around for generations. I want to shout louder than the silence. We have solidarity in our experience and strength in our collective voice. Strength we were told or forced to believe we didn't have.

It's happening all around us; our neighbor, co-worker, family member, best friend, those sitting next to you at church, the very people we care for and love. Why are we so good at pretending it's not happening? It was happening to me and I was the best at hiding and ignoring... it almost killed me. I want to make a difference, create discussion without shame, embarrassment or fear. The more these issues are talked about, the less room there is for the enemy to gain any more ground. Light casts out darkness. Talking reveals to us we are not alone. Communicating openly and more often will neutralize the taboo of, what is often viewed as, a difficult, scary and awkward subject. I want to talk to you... you that may know of someone going through a similar situation but don't know what to do. Talk to them, even if it's hard for you both. Listen and let them trust you - over time they'll come around. I want to talk to you, you the one silently hurting and living out your abuser's selfish plan for your life. God sees you and wants to help. We must let Him. We have to let others. You don't have to live in fear. I know, firsthand, how scary the thought of reaching out is. It means change, facing the unknown, and even battling the threats and intimidation that have you believing you can't leave. You see, if we challenge life and the wrong that's being done, if we can find the courage to believe in ourselves, if we can build the strength to take action - then no one can keep us from finding our true purpose in life. I've been there. I don't view you as weak or stupid... no, how wrong that would be. You're a survivor. If you're strong enough to endure and keep going each day, then you're equally strong enough to change it. It'll take some help so don't be afraid to ask. There are many organizations that will support your choice to be free of abuse. Be smart about it... you don't have to do it alone.

People asked me, they saw it on my face and noticed my demeanor... but I chose to stay silent. If you're living it, I'm sure you understand why. So, maybe it's overstepping to request something more of you, but I have to. Because when I finally did break my silence - my life got better. I must at least suggest, if you know or believe something is wrong that you'll ask the person and keep asking. And if you're the one being asked, say something. You'll both have to be brave. It can seem embarrassing or awkward - but we all go through hard times, and life challenges. We all have "things" that we would rather not tell others about. I really do understand; there's a stigma attached to abuse that doesn't belong. We internalize it and even think thoughts like, "I must have caused it" or "I don't want to be that person. People will talk and stare" or "I'm so weak and pathetic" or "I can't believe I'm letting this happen" or "He'll change" or "I have no options" - self shaming and confining thoughts... it makes no sense unless you're living it. We believe it. I believed it. It's like a child believing they're at fault when parents split up. No sane parent would allow that thinking to continue. I'm not judging - I have no right nor does anyone else. Why is judgment from anyone even on the table? It's time we all take the time to really listen. I know I'll be listening - I want to be a part of the solution.

I didn't share because I was unsure of a lot of things; would there be support for me to begin with, and then later for my children. The old saying, "the devil you know instead of the one you don't" rang true for me. I was afraid of the unknown. Some might say that makes me a coward; they're part of the problem. I'm a survivor... with a plan. My plan includes supporting a new social standard that doesn't shame or blame but encourages a healthy forum that speaks out against abuse in all its forms. I believe in a society that truly looks after one another... it's happening. We have to embrace it. I feel fortunate and grateful that I got out. I didn't do it alone; I had God, Dr. Bill, friends and family.

Who knows what my life would have been like had I not met My Past? Who knows? Doesn't really matter because I trust God's word, and it tells me, "We know that all things work together for good to them that love God, to them who are called according to *his* purpose." - Ro. 8:28. I stand on that.

What I've learned is that it's never too late to be happy and back on the road to your life plan. All the choices I've made, good and bad have led me to this place... and I'm happy, fulfilled. There's a plan for each one of us... we must discover what that is. There are few things in this life that can be guaranteed. I've found at least one; our life was given to us to have meaning. It's not meant to be lived at the hands of someone else's abuse or twisted control issues. That's not God's plan for us. I can attest to that. My life has taken a turn for the better; I have a true relationship with Jesus, I'm happily re-married, I have a whole bunch of grandchildren, great relationships with all my children, and a community of friends I love and they love me - for who I am. I am joyful... and cranky depends on the day you catch me. But at least I'm me.

It's hard to really help each other, that's the truth. It takes a steadfast commitment, that's the truth. It's all worth it. That's the truth.

I hope we'll at least try. That's all any of us can ever really do. But let's try hard.

CPSIA information can be obtained
at www.ICGtesting.com
Printed in the USA
FSHW020409180920
73440FS